WRITE RIGHT!

WRITE RIGHT!

A Canadian desk-drawer digest of punctuation, grammar, and style

Jan Venolia

Self-Counsel Press
(a division of)
International Self-Counsel Press Ltd.
Canada   U.S.A.

Printed in Canada

First edition: October, 1980
Second edition: April, 1983
Third edition: March, 1992; Reprinted: August, 1993
Fourth edition: January, 1995

Canadian Cataloguing in Publication Data

Venolia, Jan, 1928-
Write right!
(Self-counsel reference series)
Includes bibliographical references and index.
ISBN 1-55180-000-4

 1. English language — Grammar. 2. English language —
Punctuation. I. Title. II. Series.
PE1112.V46 1995   808' .042   C95-910013-X
A U.S. edition of this book has been published by Ten Speed Press.

Self-Counsel Press
(a division of)
International Self-Counsel Press Ltd.

Head and Editorial Office	*U.S. Address*
1481 Charlotte Road	1704 N. State Street
North Vancouver, British Columbia	Bellingham, Washington
V7J 1H1	98225

Table of Contents

PLEASE READ THIS FIRST:

Our language is alive — maybe not always alive and well, but alive and kicking. Its vitality shows in its ability to change and accommodate. In the decade since *Write Right!* first appeared, our vocabularies have absorbed new words (miniseries, carryon), and old words have acquired new guises (nouns have become verbs, and vice versa). Some words have taken on new meanings, occasionally rendering them more useful, but more often losing their original nuances. Conventions of grammar and usage have been altered, abandoned, and occasionally vigorously defended.

My goal in this edition of *Write Right!* is to point out some of these changes, suggesting areas where traditional usage has value and others where relaxing the rules benefits us all. *Write Right!* originally grew from two observations I made during my years as a freelance writer and editor: Certain types of grammatical errors occur repeatedly, and improvement in those areas alone markedly improves the quality of writing. The present edition retains this emphasis while taking a look at some recent changes in the language.

> *Language rests upon use; anything used long enough by enough people will become standard.* — Charlton Laird

George Orwell described language as "an instrument which we shape for our own purposes." Consider the way you use language as a vote, as your way of resisting change or demanding it — in short, of exercising some control over what becomes standard.

Write Right! guides you through the standards of good writing, making the rules accessible for everyday use. As you skim through the pages to become familiar with what is covered, note the Glossary in the back of the book; it should help you understand any unfamiliar terms. Note also that I often substitute examples for textbook style rules in order to clarify a point. Between the examples and the Glossary, you should be able to grasp any rule that isn't immediately obvious. If you have a question that is not answered in these pages, check the books listed in the Bibliography.

Confused and Abused Words may be one of the most useful chapters in the book. It sorts out pairs of words such as *affect* and *effect, fewer* and *less*; it brings you up to date on the status of words like *enthuse* and *hopefully.* The correct choice in such matters bears directly on the professional appearance of your writing.

If you are familiar with my books, you know that I am fond of quotations. This edition provides some new ones for those who share my enthusiasm and have asked for more. While enjoying the words of Mark Twain or George Bernard Shaw, remember that they illustrate rules or provide insights into good writing.

Good writing gives you ample room for self-expression; its rules never demand ambiguity or awkwardness as the price of communication. If you feel forced to choose between awkwardness and error, you can probably revise to avoid both.

As I reviewed the changes in our language, I was impressed that good writing today strives to make the reader's job easier, clearing away distracting clutter and obstacles. I hope you find *Write Right!* an ally in this task.

> *Writing is easy. All you have to do is cross out the wrong words.* — Mark Twain

Punctuation Pointers

PUNCTUATION POINTERS

Contemporary usage calls for just enough punctuation to keep the reader moving effortlessly through a sentence. Good punctuation tells the reader what is important, which items belong together, when to pause, and whether something is omitted. Incorrect punctuation, on the other hand, can mislead, distort meaning, and interrupt the flow of ideas.

Your choice of punctuation is usually determined by what you want to say or emphasize. If you keep in mind that your goal is to help the reader understand your meaning, many of your choices become automatic.

When you find a sentence particularly hard to punctuate, the problem may not be punctuation but writing style. Rewriting a basically flawed sentence may be your best alternative.

> *The workmanlike sentence almost punctuates itself.* —
> Wilson Follett

APOSTROPHE

1. **Use an apostrophe to indicate possession.**

   a) With singular words, regardless of final consonant, and with plural words that do not end in *s,* **add** *'s.*

writer's cramp	the witness's testimony
a dog's life	NHL's restrictions
children's hour	the employee's paycheck

   Canada's climate is nine months winter and three months late fall. — Evan Esar

With the exception of ancient proper names, which receive the apostrophe only, this rule applies to proper nouns.

Joyce Wieland's painting	Bruce Cockburn's music
Jesus' disciples	Achilles' heel

b) With plural words that end with _s_, add only an apostrophe.

the Davises' vacation	the flight attendants' duties
writers' conference	employees' union
the Morrises' house	the witnesses' testimony

Psychiatry enables us to correct our faults by confessing our parents' shortcomings. — Laurence J. Peter

Be sure you have the plural form of the word before you add the apostrophe; the Morrises' house, not the Morris' house or the Morris's house.

Note: the pronoun _its, his, theirs, yours, ours,_ and _whose_ are already possessive and do not need an apostrophe to show possession.

The land is ours (_not_ our's)

We have an epidemic of surplus apostrophes: Tomato's for sale, 'till, Yankee's Go Home. The mistake of adding an apostrophe to the possessive pronoun _its_ is particularly common — and it broadcasts the ignorance of the writer. Remember that an apostrophe in the word _it's_ indicates a contraction of _it is_ or _it has._

It's not easy to put the apostrophe in its place.

---

c) If possession is common to two or more individuals, add '_s_ to the last name only.

Tom and Dick's boat (_not_ Tom's and Dick's boat)

But if possession is not common, make each noun possessive.

the secretary's and the treasurer's reports

d) Treat possessives of compound words as follows:

In *singular* compound words, add '*s* to the end of the last word.

father-in-law's will   notary public's signature

With *plural* compound words, use an *of* phrase to show possession.

   the meeting of the attorneys general

   (*not* the attorneys general's meeting)

(See Rule 57d regarding formation of compound words.)

e) Use ' or '*s* in established idiomatic phrases even though ownership is not involved.

two dollars' worth   a month's vacation
a stone's throw   today's jittery market
five years' experience (or five years of experience)

Sometimes a hyphenated form is better: a two-week vacation.

f) Avoid using '*s* in the following cases:

With titles:

Poor: *The Apprenticeship of Duddy Kravitz*'s ending

Better: the ending of *The Apprenticeship of Duddy Kravitz*

With acronyms:

Poor: CFS' (CFS's) policies

Better: CFS policies

Although the possessive '*s* is often correct with inanimate objects (state's rights, the law's effect), use an *of* phrase where the possessive would be awkward.

Poor: the Tower of London's interior

Better: the interior of the Tower of London

Where usage is more descriptive than possessive, omit the apostrophe.

Actors Equity	Teachers College
printers union	citizens band radio
United Nations vote	United States foreign policy

Follow established usage in proper names.

Queenston Heights   St. Patrick's Day   Niagara Falls

2. **Use an apostrophe in contractions to indicate omission of letters or numbers.**

> summer of '42, can't, won't, he's, they're

> *I'm not denyin' the women are foolish: God Almighty made 'em to match the men.* — George Eliot

> *He hasn't a single redeeming vice.* — Oscar Wilde

Most contractions are inappropriate in formal writing, but you should use them to avoid a stilted or to create a friendly tone.

Formal, somewhat stilted: We are sure that is all the time you will need.

More casual: We are sure that's all the time you will need.

> *or*

> We're sure that's all the time you will need.

If you have any doubts about a contraction, mentally return it to its uncontracted form to see if the sentence makes sense.

> you're welcome (you are welcome),

> *not* your welcome

3. **Use an apostrophe with nouns that are followed by a gerund (see Glossary for definition of gerund).**

The plane's leaving on time amazed us all.

Six weeks in a cast was the result of Donna's skiing.

4. **Use an apostrophe to form the following plurals:**

    a) abbreviations that have periods

    M.D.'s

    b) letters where addition of *s* **alone would be confusing**

    p's and q's

    c) words used merely as words without regard to their meaning

    Don't give me any *if's, and's,* or *but's.*

The expression *do's* and *dont's* is a special case that illustrates the need to be flexible. Add an apostrophe to the word *do* when making it plural, because *dos* without the apostrophe is confusing. Add only *s* to don't, because it already has an apostrophe, and two apostrophes create a strange-looking word (*don't's*).

COLON

The colon is a mark of anticipation, as the following rules illustrate.

5. **Use a colon before a list, summary, long quotation, or final clause that explains or amplifies preceding matter. Capitalize the first letter following the colon only if it begins with a complete statement, a quotation, or more than one sentence. (See Rule 48.)**

    In two words: im possible. — Samuel Goldwyn

    A wise statesman once said: The art of taxation consists in so plucking the goose as to obtain the largest amount of feathers with the least possible amount of hissing.

9

Marriage may be compared to a cage: The birds outside despair to get in and those within despair to get out. — Montaigne

6. Use a colon following a phrase in which the words *as follows* or *the following* are either expressed or implied.

The ingredients of a diplomat's life have been identified as follows: protocol, alcohol, and Geritol.

Many hazards await the unwary consumer: deceptive packaging, misleading labels, and shoddy workmanship.

7. Use a colon in the following situations:

a) in formal salutations

Dear Mrs. Evans:

b) in ratios

3:1

c) to indicate dialogue

Margaret Fuller: I accept the universe

Thomas Carlyle: Gad! She'd better!

Note: Do not use a colon when the items of a list come immediately after a verb or preposition:

Wrong: The job requirements are: typing, shorthand, and bookkeeping.

Right: The job requirements are typing, shorthand, and bookkeeping.

COMMA

When you have trouble getting the commas right, chances are you're trying to patch up a poorly structured sentence. — Claire Kehrwald Cook

8. **Use a comma to separate independent clauses that are joined by such co-ordinating conjunctions as** *but, nor, for, yet,* **and** *so.* **(An independent clause, also known as a main clause, makes a complete statement.)**

> *The optimist proclaims that we live in the best of all possible worlds, and the pessimist fears this is true.* — James Branch Cabell

> *I respect faith, but doubt is what gets you an education.* — Wilson Mizner

Unless a comma is required to prevent misreading, you may omit it between short, closely related clauses.

> *Keep your face to the sunshine and you cannot see the shadow.* — Helen Keller

> *We are born princes and the civilizing process turns us into frogs.* — Eric Berne

If the clauses are long and contain commas, use a semicolon rather than a comma to separate them.

> *If a man begins with certainties, he shall end in doubts; but if he will be content to begin with doubts, he shall end in certainties.* — Francis Bacon

Use a comma between dependent and main clause only when the dependent clause precedes the main clause. (Dependent clauses are

11

incomplete statements that cannot stand alone; they are underlined in the following examples.)

> *If you can't say anything good about someone*, *sit right here by me.* — Alice Roosevelt Longworth

> *As scarce as truth is*, *the supply has always been in excess of demand.* — Josh Billings

> *By the time the youngest children have learned to keep the house tidy*, *the oldest grandchildren are on hand to tear it to pieces.* — Christopher Morley

a) The comma is optional when two independent clauses are joined by the conjunctions *and* **or** *or.*

> *A little sincerity is a dangerous thing, and a great deal of it is absolutely fatal.* — Oscar Wilde

> *Give a little love to a child and you get a great deal back.* — John Ruskin

The comma is omitted if the statements are short and closely related.

> *The wise make proverbs and fools repeat them.*
> — Isaac D'Israeli

> *Power tends to corrupt and absolute power corrupts absolutely.* — Lord Acton

Note: Do not use a comma before *and* or *or* unless there is a complete statement on each side of the conjunction.

Wrong: I resented his interference, and her superior smile. (her superior smile is not a complete statement)

Right: *The optimist proclaims that we live in the best of all possible worlds, and the pessimist fears this is true.* — James Branch Cabell

b) Do not use a comma between an independent and a dependent clause. (Dependent clauses are incomplete statements that could not stand alone; the dependent clauses in the following examples are underlined.)

> *Facts do not cease to exist <u>because they are ignored</u>.* —
> Aldous Huxley

> *A fanatic is one <u>who can't change his mind and won't change the subject</u>.* — Attr. to Winston Churchill

> *The art of medicine consists of amusing the patient <u>while nature cures the disease</u>.* — Voltaire

> *Old age isn't so bad <u>when you consider the alternative</u>.*
> — Maurice Chevalier

9. **Use commas to separate three or more items in a series.**

Whether to use a final comma in a series — a, b, and c versus a, b and c — has been alternately optional and required as language styles have changed. Current usage makes the final comma mandatory.

> *Writing is just having a sheet of paper, a pen, and not a shadow of an idea of what you're going to say.*
> — Françoise Sagan

> *Early to rise and early to bed*
> *Makes a man healthy, wealthy, and dead.*
> — Ogden Nash

Using the final comma gives equal weight to each item and avoids confusion. The following comma gives equal weight to each item and avoids confusion. The following sentence illustrates how an omitted final comma can create ambiguity.

> The 15-member marching band, a drum major carrying the flag and 20 Girl Guides were all part of the Canada Day parade.

The elements in the series may be short independent clauses.

> *The only way to keep your health is to eat what you don't want, drink what you don't like, and do what you'd rather not.* — Mark Twain

When the elements in the series are joined by conjunctions such as *and* or *or,* omit the commas.

> *As soon as questions of will or decision or reason or choice of action arise, human science is at a loss.* — Noam Chomsky

10. Use commas between consecutive adjectives that modify the same noun.

> an expensive, wasteful program

> *Conscience is a small, still voice that makes minority reports.* — Franklin P. Jones

Not all consecutive adjectives modify the same noun. In the following examples the first adjective modifies the combination created by the second adjective and the noun. In such cases, omit the comma.

average urban voter	cold roast beef
white tennis shoes	short time span

An easy way to determine if an adjective modifies only a noun instead of the combination of adjective and noun is to insert the word *and* between the two adjectives. "Expensive and wasteful" works but "white and tennis" doesn't. Use a comma only between those adjectives where *and* would be plausible.

The phrase "an ugly, old fur coat" illustrates both the use of a comma and its omission. "Ugly and old" sounds right, but "old and fur coat" doesn't; hence, only *ugly* and *old* are separated by a comma.

11. Use commas where needed for clarity.

a) to separate identical or similar words

Whatever you do, do well.

b) to provide a pause or avoid confusion

If he chooses, Williams can take over the program.

Once you understand, the reason is clear.

c) to indicate omission of a word or words

When angry, count ten before you speak: if very angry, a hundred. — Thomas Jefferson

12. Use a comma to set off certain elements.

a) contrasting words or phrases

Advice is judged by results, not by intentions. — Cicero

The fool wonders, the wise man asks.
— Benjamin Disraeli

The less you write, the better it must be. — Jules Renard

b) phrases that are parenthetical, disruptive, or out of order

Pessimism, when you get used to it, is just as agreeable as optimism. — Arnold Bennett

Great blunders are often made, like large ropes, of a multitude of fibers. — Victor Hugo

Every man is, or hopes to be, an idler. — Samuel Johnson

c) appositive phrases

(Appositives are nouns or phrases that are placed next to a word to provide identification or additional information.)

> Marshall McLuhan, author of *The Medium is the Massage,* calls language a form of organized stutter.

> Stuart Keate, former publisher of the *Vancouver Sun,* once wrote that Canada is the vichyssoise of nations — cold, half-French, and difficult to stir.

d) descriptive phrases or clauses that are nonrestrictive

> *(Nonrestrictive phrases add information that is not essential to the meaning of the sentence or necessary for identification.)*

> My daughter, who is a pilot, enjoys classical music.

The above example is punctuated correctly if the writer has only one daughter. But if the writer has more than one daughter, the phrase who is a pilot is essential for identification, and the commas must be omitted.

The underlined phrases in the following examples are restrictive (i.e., they tell *which* life, *which* hand, or *which* person) — thus, no commas are appropriate. Notice how omission of the restrictive phrases would distort the meaning of the sentences or leave them meaningless.

> *The life which is unexamined is not worth living.* — Plato

> *The hand that rocks the cradle is the hand that rules the world.* — William Wallace

> *A Canadian is somebody who knows how to make love in a canoe.* — Pierre Berton

16

e) introductory words, phrases, or clauses

> *Contrary to popular belief, English women do not wear tweed nightgowns.* — Hermione Gingold

> *In general, the art of government consists in taking as much money as possible from one class of citizens to give to the other.* — Voltaire

> *Meanwhile, the meek are a long time inheriting the earth.* — Bob Edwards

In the following examples, commas have been omitted to demonstrate how helpful they can be to the reader.

> As discussed earlier discharges were highly toxic.

> Every since John has regretted his decision.

> After eating the tigers dozed off.

Insert the commas correctly, and you will save the reader having to read the sentences twice.

f) dependent clauses that precede the main clause

> *If fifty million people say a foolish thing, it is still a foolish thing.* — Anatole France

> *Though familiarity may not breed contempt, it takes the edge off admiration.* — William Hazlitt

> *If at first you don't succeed, don't take any more chances.* — Kin Hubbard

13. **Use a comma between words that demand a pause or might otherwise be misunderstood.**

> Whatever you do, do well.

> To Ross, Hunter remained insulting.

Out of sight, out of mind.

14. Use a comma to set off a direct address.

> *No, Agnes, a Bordeaux is not a house of ill-repute.*
> — George Bain

> *To lose one parent, Mr. Worthing, may be regarded as a misfortune; to lose both looks like carelessness.*
> — Oscar Wilde

15. Use a comma to set off a direct quotation from the rest of the sentence.

> Admiral Farragut said, "Damn the torpedoes!"

> *"Take some more tea," the March Hare said to Alice, very earnestly. "I've had nothing yet," Alice replied in an offended tone, "so I can't take more." "You mean you can't take less," said the Hatter. "It's very easy to take more than nothing."* — Lewis Carroll

(See Rule 32 regarding other punctuation of quotations.)

16. Use a comma to indicate omission of a word or words.

> *A man likes you for what he thinks you are; a woman, for what you think she is.* — Ivan Panin

(The phrase *likes you* is omitted from the second half of the sentence.)

> *It takes a little talent to see clearly what lies under one's nose, a good deal of it to know in which direction to point that organ.* — W.H. Auden

17. Use a comma following the words *for example, that is, namely,* **and their abbreviations (e.g., i.e., viz.). Punctuation preceding these words depends on the strength of the pause you desire.**

One era's artifacts becomes another's source of antiques; for example, moustache cups and chamberpots.

A liking for the primary colors (i.e., red, yellow, and blue) is considered a sign of mental health.

18. **The comma following conjunctive adverbs (such as** *accordingly, furthermore, however, therefore, thus, indeed, nevertheless,* **and** *consequently*) **is optional, depending on whether you wish to indicate a pause.**

Sales have dropped precipitously; furthermore, employee morale has reached a new low.

Grammar books frequently do not explain rules of usage so they can be understood; indeed they are sometimes entirely useless!

I think I think; therefore, I think I am. — Ambrose Bierce

Any man's death diminishes me, because I am involved in Mankind; and therefore never send to know for whom the bell tolls, it tolls for thee. — John Donne

19. **Where not to use the comma.**

Although commas can help the reader understand your meaning, a sentence that is overloaded with commas creates a choppy, abrasive effect that slows down and antagonizes the reader. As with all punctuation marks, if you use commas sparingly and correctly, you will find that you are using them effectively.

Here are some places where commas do *not* belong:

a) Do not use a comma between two independent clauses unless they are joined by a conjunction.

Wrong: The Dow Jones Industrial Average hit a new high, the dollar continued to climb in foreign markets.

19

This error is called a comma fault, because the writer is asking too much of the comma, using it where a stronger punctuation mark (period, semicolon) is required. (See Glossary.)

Remember that independent clauses are complete within themselves and could stand as separate sentences. Unless they are joined by a conjunction (*and, but, or, nor, for,* etc.) they must either be separated by a semicolon or written as two sentences.

Wrong: The product was an in-house success, it simply didn't sell.

Right: The product was an in-house success; it simply didn't sell.

The product was an in-house success. It simply didn't sell.

b) Do not separate subject and verb by a comma.

This error frequently occurs when a comma is placed *following* the last item in a series, as in the following example:

Wrong: Riding motorcycles, hang-gliding, and skydiving, were the main pastimes in her short life.

or when the subject is a phrase:

Wrong: Placing a comma between subject and verb, is incorrect.

DASH

Dashes may indicate sloppy writing.

> *Unwarranted dashes, the lazy author's when-in-doubt expedient, typify the gushy, immature, breathless style associated with adolescents' diaries.*
> — Claire Kherwald Cook

One or two dashes per page may be too many. Can you substitute another punctuation mark for the dash (such as comma, colon, parenthesis, semicolon)? Reserve the dash for its legitimate use:

providing a sharper break in continuity than commas or a weaker break than parenthesis.

A typewritten dash consists of two hyphens with no spaces between them. If you have desktop publishing capabilities, use an em dash (—) in text where the dash is in lieu of comma or parenthesis. Use an en dash (–) to indicate inclusiveness (1930–35, pp. 15–20).

20. **Use a dash for emphasis, to indicate an abrupt change, or with explanatory phrases or words.**

> *Put all your eggs in one basket — and watch that basket!*
> — Mark Twain

> *Don't worry about avoiding temptation — as you grow older, it starts avoiding you.*
> — The Old Farmer's Almanac

Use a single dash to summarize, much as you would use a colon.

> *To live is like to love — all reason is against it, and all healthy instinct for it.* — Samuel Butler

Use a pair of dashes to enclose parenthetical elements.

> *Though motherhood is the most important of all the professions — requiring more knowledge than any other department in human affairs — there was no attention given to preparation for this office.*
> — Elizabeth Cady Stanton

ELLIPSIS

Ellipses consist of three spaced words (i.e., a space before each period and after the last).

21. **Use an ellipsis to indicate an omission within a quotation.**

> *We are told that talent creates its own opportunities.*
> *But ... intense desire creates not only its own opportuni-*
> *ties, but its own talents.* — Eric Hoffer

> *The man who ... dies rich dies disgraced.* — Andrew
> Carnegie

Use the following as a guide for spacing.

- To show omission from the middle of a sentence:

  middle ... middle

- To show omission of one or more sentences between
  sentences:

  end ... Begin

- To show omission from the middle of one sentence
  to the beginning of another sentence:

  middle ... Begin

You may use other punctuation on either side of the ellipsis dots if it
helps show what has been omitted.

> *Despite my thirty years of research into the feminine*
> *soul, I have not yet been able to answer ... the great*
> *question ... What does a woman want?*
> — Sigmund Freud

HYPHEN

22. Use a hyphen with certain prefixes and suffixes.

a) to avoid doubling or tripling a letter

re-evaluate   anti-intellectual
shell-like   pre-empt

b) if the root word begins with a capital letter

un-American   non-Euclidean
pre-Christmas   post-World War II

c) in general, with the prefixes *all-, ex-, self-, vice-,* **and with the suffix** *-elect*

      all-knowing   self-made
      ex-husband   vice-president
      president-elect   all-purpose

      Self-sacrifice enables us to sacrifice other people without blushing. — G.B. Shaw

d) to avoid awkward pronunciations or ambiguity

un-ionized   anti-nuclear
co-worker   re-read

23. Use a hyphen after a series of words having a common base that is not repeated.

      first-, second-, and third-baseman

      small- and middle-sized companies

24. Use a hyphen to form certain compound words.

      (Compound words unite two or more words, with or without a hyphen, to convey a single idea.)

The current trend is to write compound words as one word (e.g., handgun, airborne, turnkey, stockbroker). However, the hyphen should be retained in the following cases:

a) in compound nouns, where needed for clarity or as an aid in pronunciation

right-of-way   sit-in   come-on   editor-in-chief

> *Since television, the well-read are being taken over by the well-watched.* — Mortimer Adler

Omitting a needed hyphen can create confusing, and sometimes unintentionally humorous, phrases. For example, *12 hour relief* suggests that there is something called hour relief and you have 12 of them; *self storage* would be a place to store the self; *30 odd guests* might offend some of your friends.

Stopping one hyphen short of proper hyphenation is a particularly common error.

Wrong: 10-year old boy, one-to-two day delivery

Right: 10-year-old boy, one-to-two-day delivery

b) in compound adjectives (unit modifiers) when they precede the word they modify

well-to-do individual	solid-state circuit
matter-of-fact statement	twentieth-century dilemma
well-designed unit	up-to-date accounting methods

> *The authors adopted an I-can-laugh-at-it-now-but-it-was-no-laughing-matter-at-the-time attitude.*
> — Theodore Bernstein

If the words that make up the compound adjectives in the above examples *follow* the words they modify, they are no longer compound adjectives and no hyphens are used.

> The unit is well designed.

> Their accounting methods are up to date.

> *Note:* If each of the adjectives could modify the noun without the other adjective, more than a single thought is involved (i.e., it is not a compound adjective), and a hyphen is not used.
>
> a happy, healthy child
>
> a new digital alarm clock

Idiomatic usage retains the hyphen in certain compounds regardless of the order in which they appear in the sentence.

> Tax-exempt bonds can be purchased.
>
> The bonds are tax-exempt.

c) with improvised compounds

know-it-all   stick-in-the-mud
Johnny-come-lately   do-it-yourselfer

He spoke with a certain what-is-it in his voice, and I could see that if not actually disgruntled, he was far from being gruntled. — P.G. Wodehouse

The *Stylebook* prepared by the Canadian Press has a helpful section on the hyphen that indicates whether compounds words would be written as one word, two words, or hyphenated.

> *Note:* Never form a hyphenated with a word ending in *-ly*.
>
> newly formed company   widely known facts

25. Use a hyphen in fractions and compound numbers from 21 to 99.

three-fourths   thirty-seven
one-third   forty-two

26. Use a hyphen to combine numeral-unit adjectives.

12-inch ruler   5-cent cigar
30-day month   100-year lifespan

27. Use a hyphen to combine an initial capital letter with a word.

T-shirt   X-rated
U-turn   V-neck

28. Use a hyphen to divide a word at the right-hand margin.
(See Rules 62-64).

(See Rule 49b regarding capitalization of hyphenated words.)

PARENTHESES

29. Use parentheses to set off explanatory or peripheral matter.

> *It is only in good writing that you will find how words are best used, what shades of meaning they can be made to carry, and by what devices (or lack of them) the reader is kept going smoothly or bogged down.*
> — Jacques Barzun

If the parenthetical matter has a close logical relationship to the rest of the sentence, use commas instead.

> *It is probably safe to say that, over a long period of time, political morality has been as high as business morality.* — Henry Steele Commanger

30. Punctuate sentences with parentheses as follows:

a) When the parenthetical matter is a complex statement, enclose associated punctuation within the parentheses.

26

(How I wish he would!)

(Events later confirmed his suspicions.)

b) When a parenthetical item falls in the middle or at the end of a sentence, place the necessary punctuation *after* the closing parenthesis.

There is only one problem (and he admits it): his chronic tardiness.

I phoned him when I arrived (as I had promised).

Do not put a comma, semicolon, or dash before an opening parenthesis.

Wrong: I phoned him when I arrived, (as I had promised) but he was not at home.

Right: I phoned him when I arrived (as I had promised), but he was not at home.

Like dashes, parentheses can be easily overused.

Parentheses ... represent an unwillingness to spend time figuring out how to put things in the most logical order.... Every random thought, every tenuous analogy gets dragged in. — Paul Robinson.

QUESTION MARK

31. Use the following guide regarding question marks:

A question mark is used at the end of a question. That much is obvious. Whether question marks are needed at the end of every request is not always so clear. A good general rule is that if the reader is expected to act instead of reply, no question mark is necessary.

27

Will you please send me a one-year subscription.

But if you feel the request is too presumptuous as a statement, use a question mark.

Will you please feed the cat while I'm away?

QUOTATION MARKS

32. **Use quotation marks for a direct quotation (i.e., the exact words),**

> *"I'm world-famous," Dr. Parks said, "all over Canada."* — Mordecai Richler

but not an indirect one (i.e., a rearrangement or restatement of the person's words).

> Pascal said that most of the disorders and evils in life are the result of man's inability to sit still and think.

Do not use quotation marks for an indirect quotation (that is, a rearrangement or restatement).

> According to Mark Twain you should never put off till tomorrow what you can do the day after tomorrow.

When the quotation consists of several paragraphs, place a quotation mark at the beginning of each paragraph and at the end of the final paragraph.

You can also indicate a long passage of quoted material by indenting and single-spacing the text; in this case, omit quotation marks at the beginning and end of the passage.

33. **Use quotation marks to enclose a word or phrase that is defined.**

> The word "ventana" is Spanish for window.

28

"Qualifying small businesses" means those with fewer than 250 employees.

34. Use quotation marks to enclose words or phrases following such terms as *entitled, the word(s), the term, marked, designated, classified, named, endorsed,* or *signed.*

The cheque was endorsed "John Hancock."

The word "impossible" is not in my dictionary.
— Napoleon

35. Use quotation marks to indicate a misnomer or special meaning for a word.

Some "antiques" would more accurately be described as junk.

You may be sure that when a man begins to call himself a "realist," he is preparing to do something he is secretly ashamed of doing. — Sydney Harris

It is easy to overdo this usage, resulting in a cloying, affected style.

Note: Do not use quotation marks following the words *known as, called, so-called,* etc. unless the expressions that follow are misnomers or slang.

Most of our so-called reasoning consists in finding arguments for going on believing as we already do. — James Harvey Robinson

---

36. Use quotation marks to enclose titles of component parts of whole publications: chapters or other divisions of a book; articles in periodicals; songs; stories, essays, poems, and the like, in anthologies or similar collections.

"Birches"

"Punctuation Pointers"

Titles of *whole* published works such as books, periodicals, plays, and reports should be underlined or italicized.

Write Right!

The London Free Press

37. Use punctuation associated with quotation marks as follows:

Place comma and final period *inside* the quotation marks; place other punctuation marks *outside* the quotation marks unless they are part of the material being quoted.

> *You've heard of the three ages of man: youth, middle age, and "You're looking wonderful!"*
> — Cardinal Spellman

She had the audacity to answer "No"!

Who asked "Why?"

Do you think we should watch "News Hour"?

Charts answer the question "how much," maps answer the question "where," and diagrams answer the question "how."

> *"My country, right or wrong" is like saying "My mother, drunk or sober."* — G.K. Chesterton

38. Use single quotation marks to indicate a quote within a quote.

> Kin Hubbard wrote: "When a fellow says, 'It ain't the money but the principle of the thing,' it's the money."

SEMICOLON

Some writers today are fond of semicolons, while others discourage their use.

It is almost always a greater pleasure to come across a semicolon than a period.... You get a pleasant feeling of expectancy; there is more to come; read on; it will get clearer. — George F. Will

Semicolons are pretentious and overactive.... Far too often, [they] are used to gloss over an imprecise thought. They place two clauses in some kind of relationship to one another, but relieve the writer of saying exactly what the relationship is. — Paul Robinson

39. Use a semicolon between independent clauses that are too closely related to be written as separate sentences.

Children begin by loving their parents; as they grow older they judge them; sometimes they forgive them. — Oscar Wilde

It is with narrow-souled people as with narrow-necked bottles; the less they have in them, the more noise they make in pouring out. — Alexander Pope

A neurotic is the man who builds a castle in the air; a psychotic is the man who lives in it; and a psychiatrist is the man who collects the rent. — Lord Webb-Johnson

40. Use a semicolon to separate a series of phrases that already contain commas.

The meeting was attended by Lloyd Harrison, president of the board; Evelyn White, chief delegate of the consumer groups; William Blake, representing the press; and Preston Tracy, speaking for the shareholders.

41. Use a semicolon preceding explanatory phrases introduced by words such as *for example, that is,* or *namely* when you want a stronger break than a comma would provide.

Secretaries have many unpopular assignments; for example, making coffee.

31

42. Use a semicolon between independent clauses that are long or contain commas.

> *Copy from one, it's plagiarism; copy from two, it's research.* — Wilson Mizner

> *Doing business without advertising is like winking at a girl in the dark; you know what you are doing, but nobody else does.* — S. Britt

---

Note: The conjunctive adverb *however* seems to invite punctuation errors. The difficulty appears to be the assumption that *however* and a pair of commas are sufficient to glue together two independent clauses. Instead, the result is a *comma fault.* (See Glossary.) Two independent clauses joined by *however* require a complete stop (either a semicolon or a period).

Wrong: Projections were gloomy, however, sales skyrocketed.

Right: Projections were gloomy; however, sales skyrocketed.

A comma follows *however* whenever it is an interruption or suggests contrast with something preceding it — which is most of the time. But when *however* is used in the sense of "no matter how," no comma is used.

Let him step to the music which he hears, however measured or far away. — Thoreau

---

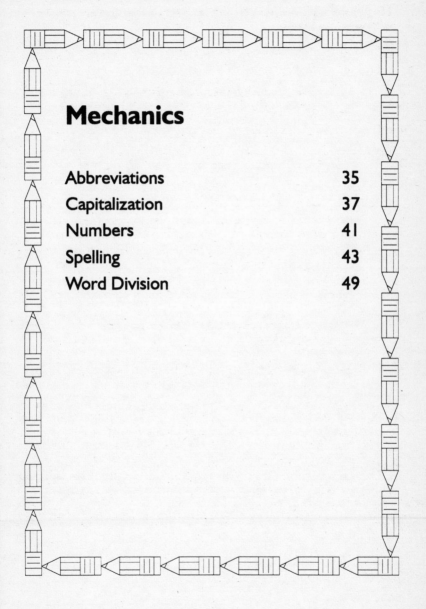

Mechanics

MECHANICS

ABBREVIATIONS

A good rule of thumb for formal writing is *Don't abbrev*. However, when abbreviations are appropriate, as in company names, military titles, outside addresses, and footnotes, be sure to use them correctly.

43. **The preferred abbreviation for a province (or a state) in an outside address is two capital letters and no period.**

Alberta AB	Nova Scotia NS
British Columbia BC	Ontario ON
Manitoba MB	Prince Edward Island PE
New Brunswick NB	Quebec PQ
Newfoundland NF	Saskatchewan SK
Northwest Territories NT	Yukon YT

Do not abbreviate inside addresses (i.e., those typed on the first page of the letter).

44. **Social titles are usually abbreviated *(Ms., Mrs., Mr.)*. The correct (formal) plural of the abbreviation of *Mr.* is *Messrs.* and of *Mrs.* is *Mmes.***

The debate over using *Ms.* instead of *Miss* or *Mrs.* has largely subsided, leaving us with a useful, marital-status-free title. *Ms.* is now acceptable in both business and social contexts; however, use *Miss* or *Mrs.* when you know an individual prefers it.

Abbreviate other titles only when you use the person's full name.

> Gen. Frances Fyte

> Rev. Sam Soule

If the full name is not used, do not abbreviate the title. Similarly, a full date can be abbreviated (Dec. 7, 1941), but a partial date should be written in full (December 7, *not* Dec. 7).

45. When an abbreviated word is also a contraction, do not use an apostrophe to indicate the contraction.

> Intl., *not* Int'l (for International)

46. Use an apostrophe to form the plural of an abbreviation that has periods.

> Seventy-three M.D.'s attended the meeting.

47. Observe the following usages in footnoted or parenthetical matter.

Abbreviate foreign words only when they appear in footnotes or parentheses. Since many people are not familiar with the foreign words from which their abbreviations are derived, the shortened versions may be a confusing jumble of letters. They are often incorrectly punctuated as well. You avoid such problems by writing out *for example, that is,* and *namely* when they appear in text. Be sure to separate them from what follows with a comma.

Replace:	with:
e.g.	for example
i.e.	that is
viz.	namely

CAPITALIZATION

Approach capitalization not as a rigid set of rules to be mastered, but as a flexible instrument of style. The primary function of capitals is to make your meaning clear; observing the following conventions will help you achieve that goal.

48. Capitalize the first word after a colon in the following cases:

a) if the material following the colon is a formal rule or a complete statement that expresses the main thought

> The company has a new policy: Every employee is given a company car.

b) if what precedes the colon is a word like *Note* or *Caution*

> Caution: Radioactive material enclosed.

49. Capitalize titles as follows:

a) In titles of books, plays, television programs, etc., capitalize the first and last words, plus all principal words.

Articles, conjunctions, and short prepositions are not capitalized unless they begin the title. Prepositions are capitalized if they consist of four or more letters or if they are connected with a preceding verb.

> Stop the World, I Want to Get Off

> Customers Held Up by Gunmen

> Situation Calls for Action

b) Capitalize both parts of a hyphenated word in a title unless it is considered as one word or is a compound numeral.

> Report of the Ninety-fifth Parliament

> Well-Known Author Dies

> Anti-inflation Measures Taken

c) Personal titles are capitalized only if they precede the name and are not separated by a comma.

> Professor Reynolds

> the treasurer, Will Knott

Capitalization is optional if the title follows the noun.

> Lightfoot Walker, president of the corporation

> *or* Lightfoot Walker, President of the corporation.

50. **Capitalize both the full names and the shortened names of government agencies, bureaus, departments, services, etc.**

> Parks Branch

> Sheriff's Office

> Statistics Canada

> Bureau of Pension Advocates

> Ombudsman of B.C.

> Law Reform Commission

Do not capitalize the words *government, federal, administration,* etc. except when part of the title of a specific entity.

> The Canadian Government is the largest employer in the nation.

> She hopes to work for the federal government.

Capitalization of departments or divisions of a company is optional.

> Claims Department, *or* claims department

> Engineering Division, *or* engineering division

51. Capitalize points of the compass and regional terms when they refer to specific sections or when they are part of a precise descriptive title,

the East	Vancouver's West End
the Western Hemisphere	Eastern Europe

but not merely suggesting direction or position.

western provinces	south of town
east coast	northern lights

Go west, young man. — John B.L. Soule

Some regional terms, such as *Prairie Provinces,* seem to be either part of a "precise descriptive title" or "merely suggest position," depending on your viewpoint. Since authorities can be found on both sides of this gray area, I suggest you choose whichever you are more comfortable with, and capitalize accordingly.

52. **Capitalize abbreviations, if the words they stand for are capitalized.**

M.D.   M.P.
Ph.D.   M.L.A.

53. **Capitalize ethnic groups, factions, alliances, and political parties, but not the word** *party,* **itself.**

> He spoke for the Chinese community.

> The Liberal party held its convention in July.

> The Communist bloc vetoed the proposal.

Note: Political groupings other than parties are usually lowercased:

He represents the left wing of the Canadian Labor Congress.

But:

the Right, the Left

Negro and *Caucasian* are always capitalized, but blacks, whites, or slang words for the races are lowercased.

---

54. **Capitalize scientific names for genus, but not species.**

> *Drosophila melanogaster (abbreviated D. melanogaster)*

> *Homo sapiens*

> *Note:* Do not capitalize the seasons.
> Do not capitalize a.m. or p.m.

NUMBERS — Figures or Words?

A few conventions regarding the writing of numbers should be observed.

55. Spell out numbers in the following cases:

a) at the beginning of a sentence

> *Fifteen men on the Dead Man's Chest.* — Robert Louis Stevenson

b) when the number is less than 10 and does not appear in the same sentence with larger numbers*

> *Sometimes I've believed as many as six impossible things before breakfast.* — Lewis Carroll

c) to represent round numbers of indefinite expressions

> several thousand people
>
> the roaring Twenties
>
> between two and three hundred employees
>
> in her eighties

d) fractions standing alone or followed by *of a* **or** *of an*

one-fourth inch   two-thirds of a cup
two one-hundredths   one-half of an apple

---

*I use here the convention adopted by the Canadian Press Style Book. Some texts state that numbers less than 100 should be written as words, but current usage favors 10 as the dividing point.

e) preceding a unit modifier that contains a figure

three 8-foot planks   six 1/2-inch strips

56. Use figures to represent numbers in the following cases:

a) when the number itself is 10 or more

b) when numbers below 10 occur with larger numbers and refer to the same general subject

> I have ordered 9 cups of coffee, 6 cups of tea, and 15 sandwiches to be delivered in one hour.

(The number *one* in "one hour" is not related to the other numbers and thus is not written as a figure.)

c) when they refer to parts of a book

Chapter 9   page 75
Table 1   Figure 5

d) when they precede units of time, measurement, or money

18 years old   2 x 4 centimetres
9 o'clock or 9:00   3 hours 30 minutes 12 seconds
$1.50   75 cents
1/4-millimetre pipe   10 litres

Note: Units of time, measurement, and money do not affect the rule determining use of figures when numbers appear elsewhere in a sentence (see Rule 56b, above). For example:

Wrong: The 3 students collected $50 apiece.

Right: The three students collected $50 apiece.

SPELLING

There is no better cure for bad spelling than a lot of good reading, with a mind alert to the appearance of the words. Frequent dictionary use is also essential. However, a few rules may prove useful.

57. Forming plurals:

a) if the noun ends in *o*

when preceded by a vowel, always add *s*

studios	cameos
kangaroos	patios
rodeos	zoos

when preceded by a consonant, usually add *es*

potatoes	innuendoes
heroes	torpedoes

but, musical terms ending in *o* add only *s*

solos	pianos
banjos	sextos

and there are other words ending in *o* where you add only *s*

radios	mementos
zeros	avocados

plus about 40 more. If in doubt, consult your dictionary.

b) nouns ending in *s, x, ch, sh,* **and** *z,* **add** *es*

boxes	beaches
bushes	bosses

c) nouns ending in *y*

when preceded by a consonant, change the *y* to *i* and add *es*

company	companies
authority	authorities
category	categories
parody	parodies

when preceded by a vowel, simply add *s*

attorney	attorneys
money	moneys*

*Moneys is the preferred plural, according to most modern diction-
aries, but it is occasionally spelled *monies.*

d) compound words

Form plurals with the principal word.

notaries public	mothers-in-law
attorneys general	major generals
deputy chiefs of staff	commanders in chief

If the words are of equal weight, make both plural.

coats of arms	men employees
secretaries-treasurers	women writers

Nouns ending with *-ful,* add *s* to the end of the word,

cupfuls	teaspoonfuls

unless you wish to convey the use of more than one container. In that case, write as two words and make the noun plural.

> cups full (separate cups)

> buckets full (separate buckets)

Note: Form possessives of **singular** compound words at the end of the last word (*mother-in-law's, attorney general's*). Indicate possessives of **plural** compound words without the use of an apostrophe (the meeting of the attorneys general, *not* the attorneys general's meeting).

---

e) acronyms, numbers, and letters

As much as possible without creating confusion, simply add *s* to plurals.

VIPs	the three Rs
in twos and threes	the late 1960s

But abbreviations with a period or lowercase letters require an apostrophe as well.

I.O.U.'s	x's and y's

f) foreign words

Certain words (primarily Latin in origin) form plurals according to their foreign derivation. Some of the most common are listed below, followed by examples of foreign words whose plural forms have become Anglicized. A recent edition of a good dictionary is your best guide.

45

Singular	Plural
alumnus (masc.)	alumni (masc. or masc. and fem.)
alumna (fem.)	alumnae (fem.)
axis	axes
crisis	crises
criterion	criteria
datum	data
medium	media
memorandum	memoranda or memorandums
nucleus	nuclei
phenomenon	phenomena
stimulus	stimuli
stratum	strata

Note the singular form of *criteria* and *phenomena*. A common mistake is the use of the plural form instead of *criterion* or *phenomenon*. The word *data* is also frequently misused. Although it is popularly treated as singular, in formal writing (especially scientific) you should treat it as the plural word it is. Thus, data *are,* not data *is.*

g) anglicized plurals

antenna	antennas
appendix	appendixes
cactus	cactuses
formula	formulas
index	indexes (scientific, use indices)
prospectus	prospectuses

58. Add suffixes as follows:

Drop the silent *e* the end of a word when adding a suffix that begins with a vowel:

age	aging	force	forceable
move	moveable	route	routing
sale	saleable	use	usage

Double the final consonant of the root word when all of the following conditions are met:

> suffix begins with a vowel:
>
>> (committed, regrettable, running)
>
> root word ends in a single consonant that is preceded by a single vowel:
>
>> swim (swimming), grin (grinned), flap (flapper)
>
> last syllable is accented, or the word consists of one syllable:
>
>> (remit, rip, put)

Exceptions: chagrined, transferable

The following words do not meet at least one of the above requirements, and thus the final consonant is not doubled:

commit   commitment
(suffix does not begin with a vowel)

appeal   appealed
(final consonant is preceded by a double vowel)

render   rendered
(last syllable is not accented)

The following words *do* meet the requirements:

bag   baggage
red   reddish
occur   occurrence
refer   referred

transfer	transferred
commit	committed

> *Note:* If the accent moves to the preceding syllable with the addition of a suffix, the final consonant is not doubled.
>
> | refer | reference |
> |--------|------------|
> | prefer | preference |

59. **Words ending in** *-able* or *-ible.*

We have no convenient, watertight rule for determining whether to add *-able* or *-ible.* But here's a slightly helpful guide:

Any words that has an *-ation* form always takes the suffix *-able.*

durable (duration)
commendable (commendation)
irritable (irritation)
excitable (excitation)

Words with *-ion, -tion, -id,* or *-ive* forms usually take the suffix *-ible.*

collectible (collection)
irresistible (resistive)
digestible (digestion)
suggestible (suggestive)

But remember this is not completely reliable. For example, some words that do not have an *-ation* form nonetheless take *-able* (manageable, desirable, likable). A dictionary will solve the problem if you are uncertain.

> *For every credibility gap there is a gullibility gap.* —
> Richard Clopton

Honesty is a good thing, but it is not profitable to its possessor unless it is kept under control. — Don Marquis

60. Words ending in -*sede,* -*ceed,* **and** -*cede.*

Only one word ends in -*sede* (supersede), and three end in -*ceed* (exceed, proceed, succeed). All other words of this type end in -*cede* (precede, secede...).

Nothing succeeds like excess. — Oscar Wilde

61. *ei* **and** *ie* **words**

The grammar school jingle we all learned has so many exceptions that you should use it only when you don't have a dictionary handy. The first line of the jingle is the more useful part.

Put *i* before *e,* except after *c,*

(*i* before *e,*): piece, brief, niece

(except after *c,*): receive, ceiling, deceive

This rule applies only when the words containing *ei* or *ie* are pronounced like *ee* (as in *need*). When the sound is other than *ee,* the correct spelling is usually *ei* (e.g., freight, vein). Some exceptions are *either/neither, seize, financier,* and *weird.*

It is a pity that Chaucer, who had geneyus, was so unedicated. He's the wuss speller I know of. — Artemus Ward

WORD DIVISION

Words that are divided at the right-hand margin are an interruption to the reader; incorrectly divided words slow the reader down even more. So divide words only when you must, and always do it correctly. Both parts of a divided word should be pronounceable, and you should avoid breaking a word so that the first fragment produces a misleading meaning (legis-lature, not leg-islature; peas-ant, not pea-sant).

62. Divide words as follows:

a) between syllables

num-ber	moun-tain
con-sonant	egg-head
know-ledge	prod-uct

Careful pronunciation will help you determine correct syllabication.

b) between double letters

quar-rel	refer-ring
com-mittee	accom-modate

unless the double letter comes at the end of the simple form of the word

call-ing	bless-ing
success-ful	add-ing

c) in hyphenated words, only where the hyphen already exists

thirty-five, not thir-ty-five

d) at a prefix or suffix, but not within it

super-market, not su-permarket

contra-ceptive, not con-traceptive

e) to produce the most meaningful grouping

careless-ness, not care-lessness

consign-ment, not con-signment

f) after a one-letter syllable

busi-ness   deli-cate
sili-con   statu-ary

unless the one-letter syllable is part of the suffixes *-able* or *-ible*

illeg-ible   mov-able
inevit-able   permiss-ible

Note: The *a* and *i* in many *-able* and *-ible* words are not one-letter syllables and should be divided as in the following examples:

ame-na-ble   pos-si-ble
ter-ri-ble   char-i-ta-ble
ca-pa-ble   swim-ma-ble

---

63. **Do not divide the following:**

a) one-syllable words

b) words with fewer than six letters

c) one-letter syllables

alone, not a-lone   eu-phoria, not euphori-a

d) two-letter syllables at the end of a word

caller, not call-er   pur-chaser, not purchas-er
walked, not walk-ed   leader, not lead-er

Another way of stating the last two rules (c and d) is that you should leave at least two letters before the hyphen and three letters after it.

e) these suffixes

-cial	-cion	-cious	-tious
-tial	-sion	-ceous	-geous
-sial	-tion	-gion	-gious

f) abbreviations, contractions, or a person's name

g) the last word of a paragraph or last word on a page

64. When three or more consonants come together, let pronunciation be your guide.

punc-ture   match-ing
chil-dren   birth-day

When in doubt, consult a dictionary, where you will find the words divided into syllables.

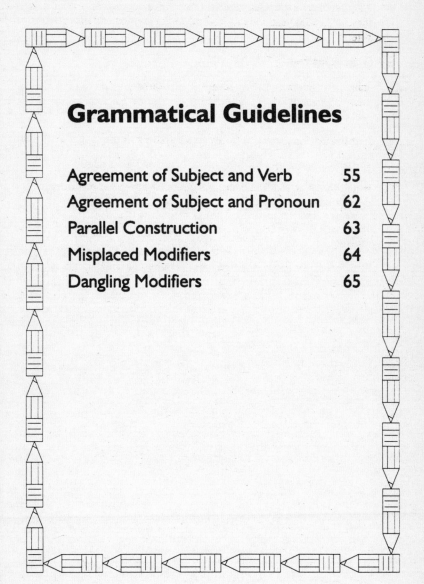

Grammatical Guidelines

GRAMMATICAL GUIDELINES

One of the best ways to get a grip on grammar is to develop an ear for the sound of properly used language. Ironically, at a time when our ears are bombarded by radio and television, your best bet for exposure to the "sound" of correct grammar still lies in the visual act of reading good prose. Read widely, and read the best of writers. You will absorb grammar and style as if through your pores.

> *Literature is simply the appropriate use of language.*
> — Evelyn Waugh

Grammar helps us to introduce order into our language. Its rules communicate the logical relationship between language and reality. If you abandon that logical, orderly relationship, you diminish your ability to communicate.

> *Languages have singulars and plurals because reality comes to us that way, and we have to have some way of dealing with that fact.* — Bruce O. Boston

65. Subject and verb must agree both in person and number.

This rule seems to top everyone's list. Jacques Barzun has some good words on the subject:

> *Agreement is as pleasant in prose as it is in personal relations, and no more difficult to work for.*

Theodore Bernstein devotes five pages to the subject in his book, *The Careful Writer.* He claims errors in agreement are the most common mistakes writers make.

On the surface, the rule seems simple: A verb must agree with its subject both in person and number. Thus, a singular subject requires a singular verb. *(Tom is late.)* A plural or compound subject requires a plural verb. *(Tom and Bill are late.)* A subject in the first person requires a verb in the first person. *(I am exasperated.)* A subject in the third person requires a verb in the third person. *(She is exasperated.)* And so on.

Applying this rule can be difficult. For example, it is not always clear which word or phrase is the subject. And even if the subject is easy to identify, it may not be clear whether it is singular or plural. The most common trouble spots regarding agreement of subject and verb are presented below in those two general categories: identifying the subject and determining the number.

a) Identifying the Subject

(1) Intervening Phrases

Phrases that come between subject and verb do not affect the number of the verb.

> The *purpose* of his speeches *was* to win votes.

> The company's total *salaries,* exclusive of overtime, *are* $2000 per week.

> *One* of the reasons he *was* late for dinner was that his watch had stopped.

The subjects of the above sentences are *purpose, salaries,* and *one,* respectively. By mentally leaving out the phrases that come between those subjects and their verbs, you can determine if a singular or plural verb is required.

(2) Phrases and Clauses as Subject

When the subject of a sentence is a phrase or clause, it takes a singular verb. The subjects of the following sentences are *The best way to keep your friends* and *What this country needs.*

The best way to keep your friends is not to give them away. — Wilson Mizner

What this country needs is a good 5¢ nickel. — F.P. Adams

(3) Inverted Sentence Order

The subject usually precedes the verb. But when the subject follows the verb, it is sometimes hard to tell if the verb should be singular or plural. In the following example, the subject is *Margaret Atwood*, not popular authors, and a singular verb is correct.

> Leading the list of popular authors was Margaret Atwood.

In the following sentences the compound subject *a group of taxpayers and their M.L.A.* requires a plural verb.

> Seeking to defeat the amendment were a group of taxpayers and their M.L.A.

First locate the subject and then you will know what the number of the verb should be.

b) Determining the Number

(1) Compound Subjects

Two subjects joined by *and* are a compound subject, and they require a plural verb.

> The title and abstract of the report are printed on the first page.

> Writing a report and filing it are difficult tasks for the new manager.

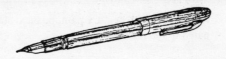

Note: The following are exceptions to the preceding rule:

If the two parts of the compound subject are regarded as one unit, they take a singular verb.

Bacon and eggs is a good way to start the day.

Compound subjects preceded by *each* or *every* are singular.

Every man, woman, and child is given full consideration.

Each nut and bolt is individually wrapped.

Company names, though they may combine several units or names, are considered as a single entity and thus take a singular verb.

Jones and Associates is a management consulting firm.

Best, Best, & Best Co. is a major department store.

(2) Collective Nouns

Nouns such as *family, couple, group, people, majority, percent,* or *personnel* take either singular or plural verbs. If the word refers to the group as a whole or the idea of oneness predominates, use a singular verb.

> The group is meeting tonight at seven.
>
> The elderly couple was the last to arrive.
>
> *A minority may be right; a majority is always wrong.* — Henrik Ibsen

But if the word refers to individuals within a group, use a plural verb.

> A group of 19th century paintings and statues were donated to the museum.

A couple of latecomers were escorted to their seats.

Similarly, words ending in *-ics* (e.g., *statistics, athletics, politics, economics*) take either singular or plural verbs, depending on their use.

> Human rights is a sensitive issue. (singular)

> Human rights are often ignored. (plural)

> Statistics is a difficult subject. (singular)

> The statistics show a decreasing birth rate. (plural)

> *Politics offers yesterday's answers to today's problems.*
> — Marshall McLuhan

The word *number* is singular when preceded by *the* and plural when precede by *a.*

> A *number* of stock market indicators *were* favorable.

> *The number* of students enrolling in college *is* decreasing.

(3) Indefinite Pronouns

The following pronouns are always singular: *another, each, every, either, neither,* and *one,* as are the compound pronouns made with *any, every, some,* and *no: anybody, anything, anyone, nobody, nothing, no one,* etc.

> *Neither* of the tax returns *was* completed correctly.

> *Each* of you *is* welcome.

> *Every dog has his day.* — Cervantes

> *Nothing is so useless as a general maxim.* — Macaulay

> *Note:* When the word *each* follows a plural subject, it does not affect the verb, which remains plural.
>
> The voters each have their own opinion.

The following pronouns are always plural: *both, few, many, others,* and *several.*

> *Many are called, but few are chosen.* — Matthew 22:14

The following pronouns are either singular or plural, depending on the noun referred to: *all, none, some, more,* and *most.*

> All the milk is gone. (singular)
>
> All the mistakes were avoidable. (plural)
>
> None of the laundry was properly cleaned. (singular)
>
> Three people were in the plane, but none was hurt. (singular)
>
> None are more lonesome than long-distance runners. (plural)

It may help to note than when *none* means "no one" or "not one," it takes a singular verb; when it means "not any" or "no amount," it takes a plural verb.

The relative pronouns *who, which,* and *that* are also either singular or plural, depending on whether the words they stand for (their antecedents) are singular or plural. This is straightforward when the pronoun immediately follows its antecedent:

> The employee who is late... (singular antecedent)
>
> The employees who are late... (plural antecedent)

An expert is one who knows more and more about less and less. — Nicholas Murray Butler

But if the sentence reads "An expert is one of those who ...," which is the antecedent of *who: those* or *one*? Virtually all authorities agree that the antecedent is *those,* thus requiring a plural verb after *who.*

Wrong: She is one of those employees who is chronically late.

Right: She is one of those employees who are chronically late.

(4) Either/or, Neither/nor Constructions

The verb is singular when the elements that are connected by *either/or* or *neither/nor* are singular:

> Neither his teacher nor his mother was able to help.

> *Neither snow, nor rain, nor heat, nor gloom of night stays these couriers from their appointed rounds.* — Herodotus

If the elements that are combined are plural, the verb is plural:

> Either personal cheques or major credit cards are satisfactory methods of payment.

If the elements combined are both singular and plural, the number of the element immediately preceding the verb determines the number of the verb:

> Neither the twins nor their cousin is coming to the party.

> *Either war is obsolete or men are.* — Buckminster Fuller

(5) Expressions of Time, Money, and Quantity

If a total amount is indicated, use a singular verb:

> Ten dollars is a reasonable price.

61

If the reference is to individual units, use a plural verb:

> Ten dollar bills are enclosed.

(6) Fractions

The number of the noun following a fraction determines the number of the verb:

> Three-fourths of the ballots have been counted. (plural)

> Three-fourths of the money is missing. (singular)

> *Democracy is the recurrent suspicion that more than half of the people are right more than half of the time.* — E.B. White

66. Make subject and pronoun agree in number.

Just as subject and verb should agree in number, so should subject and pronoun agree.

> Each student is bringing his (not *their*) own books.

> The Progressive Conservative party has nominated its (not *their*) candidate.

> The employees are bringing their (not *his* or *her*) own bag lunches.

More and more writers are looking for ways to avoid using the masculine pronouns (*he, him, his*) for both sexes. As a result, some have strayed from subject-pronoun agreement

> Almost everyone breaks this rule, don't they?

They find a long history for this usage.

> *Everybody does and says what they please.*
> — Lord Byron

It's enough to drive anyone out of their senses.
— George Bernard Shaw

Often you can avoid both grammatical error and sexism by rewriting.

It's enough to drive you out of your senses.

The employees each provide their own tools.

67. Use parallel construction.

Parallel thoughts should be expressed in grammatically parallel terms. Thus, you can have a sequence of gerunds or infinitives, but not a gerund followed by an infinitive:

Wrong: Swimming is better exercise than to ski.

Right: Swimming is better exercise than skiing.

Wrong: The students came on foot, by car, and bicycle.

Right: The students came on foot, by car, and by bicycle.

Wrong: in spring, in summer, and fall

Right: in spring, in summer, and in fall

This principle is also important in numbered lists, outlines, or headings.

Wrong:	**Right:**
1. Select the team.	1. Select the team.
2. Train the team.	2. Train the team.
3. Evaluating the team.	3. Evaluate the team.

Use parallel words, phrases, clauses, verbs, and tenses to improve the flow of ideas and heighten impact. Similarity of form helps the reader recognize similarity of content or function.

> *We think according to nature; we speak according to rules; we act according to custom.* — Francis Bacon

> *Canada has no cultural unity, no linguistic unity, no religious unity, no economic unity, no geographic unity. All it has is unity.* — Kenneth Boulding

Parallel treatment also avoids the sexist implications of handling names.

Wrong: Mr. Swanson and Lydia

Right: George Swanson and Lydia Swanson; George and Lydia

Wrong: Golda and Kissinger

Right: Golda Meir and Henry Kissinger; Mrs. Meir and Mr. Kissinger

68. Avoid misplaced modifiers.

Keep related words together and in the order that conveys the intended meaning.

> We almost lost all of the crop.

> We lost almost all of the crop.

Both are correct grammatically, but only one accurately describes the situation. To avoid this type of confusion, place adverbs directly *preceding* the word or phrase they modify.

Wrong: He told her that he wanted to marry her frequently.

Right: He frequently told her that he wanted to marry her.

Sometimes slight rewording removes the confusion.

Wrong: The seminar is designed for adolescents who have been experimenting with drugs and their parents.

Right: The seminar is designed for adolescents who have been experimenting with drugs and for their parents.

As the following examples illustrate, misplaced modifiers can produce some charming images, but your readers may be entertained at your expense.

> We saw a man on a horse with a wooden leg.

> The sunbather watched the soaring seagulls wearing a striped bikini.

> The politician met informally to discuss food prices and the high cost of living with several women.

> The fire was extinguished before any damage was done by the Fire Department.

> Be sure to purchase enough yarn to finish the sweater before you start.

69. Avoid dangling modifiers.

A dangling modifier gives the false impression that it modifies a word or group of words, but what it modifies has actually been left out of the sentence. For example:

Wrong: After writing the introduction, the rest of the report was easy.

After writing the introduction appears to modify the *rest of the report.* But obviously *the rest of the report* did not do the writing. Whoever did the writing has been omitted. Correct versions would be:

Right: After I wrote the introduction, the rest of the report was easy.

After writing the introduction, he found the rest of the report easy.

65

Some danglers are so subtle that they slip by established writers and their editors. Others are real howlers.

> Weighing the alternatives carefully, a decision was reached.

> At the age of five, his father died.

> When dipped in butter, you can taste the lobster's delicious flavor.

These should be rewritten as follows:

> Weighing the alternatives carefully, we reached a decision.

> At the age of five, the boy became an orphan.

> When dipped in butter, the lobster tastes delicious.

Dangling modifiers frequently result in ridiculous statements:

> Being old and dog-eared, I was able to buy the book for 50¢.

> Walking along the shore, a fish suddenly jumped out of the water.

Exceptions: Certain modifying phrases, though they may seem only loosely related to the words that follow, are acceptable. Examples are *all things considered, strictly speaking,* and *judging by the record.*

Some Specifics of Style

SOME SPECIFICS OF STYLE

The greatest possible merit of style is, of course, to
make the words absolutely disappear into the thought.
— Nathaniel Hawthorne

The following rules will help.

70. Omit unnecessary words.

This rule has long been the favorite of authors of style manuals. They often find the comparison with obesity irresistible, evoking such images as trimming the lard, empty calories for the mind, fat sentences, verbal junk food, and whittling away at the verbal waistline.

The rule against unnecessary words has taken on even greater importance with the increased use of word processors. The ease of writing with a word processor encourages verbosity. However, the technology that spreads the disease also provides a cure. Revising on a word processor to eliminate unnecessary words is a relatively simple procedure that you should exploit fully if it's available to you.

Beware of the attitude that equates impressiveness of writing with the length and number of words and with the opacity of sentences. If it's hard to understand, it must be profound, right? Wrong.

Wrong: Our proposal follows the sequential itemization of points occurring elsewhere in your RFP, wherever possible, to facilitate your review...

Translation: We will follow your outline.

Another source of wordiness is the redundancy and sloppy usage we have built into the language over the years. *General consensus of opinion* uses four words where only one is correct; consensus means collective opinion, general agreement, and accord. Thinking about the meaning of a word will help you remove some of the clutter surrounding it. *Unanimous* means having the agreement and consent of all; what is added by writing *completely unanimous*? How about that ubiquitous *free gift*; are there any other kinds? Although water heaters are supposed to heat cold water, the flabby phrase *hot water heater* is more often seen than the tighter, and more accurate, *water heater*.

Remove unnecessary words from expressions such as the following:

first time ever	past history
original founder	joint collaboration
regular routine	both men and women alike
unexpected surprise	ultimate outcome
sudden impulse	sum total
rarely ever	extra added features
small in size	advance warning
may possibly	temporary reprieve
present incumbent	10:00 a.m. Friday morning
two polar opposites	overused cliché

When you use the word "whether," omit "or not" if it is excess baggage.

Wordy: They couldn't decide whether or not to give all their money to charity.

Better: They couldn't decide whether to give all their money to charity.

In some cases "or not" is needed.

> *I figure you have the same chance of winning the lottery whether you play or not.* — Fran Lebowitz

"Rather" is redundant in a sentence with another comparative.

Wordy: It would be safer to destroy the chemicals rather than to store them.

Better: It would be safer to destroy the chemicals than to store them.

Omit unnecessary prepositions.

> all of the details = all the details

> finish up the work = finish the work

Leisurely openers like *There is, there are,* and *It is significant to note that* can usually be cut with no loss. *Both* is redundant in sentences where other words already convey "bothness."

Wordy: Both tulips as well as daffodils…

Better: Tulips as well as daffodils… *or*

>   Both tulips and daffodils

Trim wordy expressions such as the following:

> it is often the case that = frequently

> in the event that = if

> be of the opinion that = believe

> be in possession of = have

> owing to the fact that = since or because

> the fact that he had arrived = his arrival

> on the order of = about

> in advance of = before

> in spite of the fact that = although

> is indicative of = indicates

> had occasion to be = was

> put in an appearance = appeared

> take into consideration = consider

In the rush to put our ideas on paper, we frequently use words that are not only unnecessary but actually obscure what we are trying to convey. As with other sources of wordiness, the best cure is to revise, revise, and revise again. Edit once looking strictly for spare words. When you think you have pruned every one, review the document once more to see if you missed any.

71. Prefer the active voice.

The difference between active and passive voice is the difference between *Karen read the report* and *The report was read by Karen.*

The passive voice tends to use more words and always lacks the vigor of the active voice. Changing a sentence from passive to active usually improves it.

Passive: Hazardous reagents should never be poured into the sink.

Active: Never pour hazardous reagents into the sink.

Passive: The collision was witnessed by a pedestrian.

Active: A pedestrian witnessed the collision.

Reserve passive constructions for situations in which the thing acted upon is more important than the person performing the action (The meeting was cancelled), in technical material (The test apparatus was divided into two zones), or where anonymity of those performing the action is appropriate (The information was leaked to the press).

72. If appropriate, use a positive form.

Stating things positively often helps the reader get the right picture. Watch for the word *not* and see if you can restate the idea more effectively.

Negative: He often did not arrive on time.

Positive: He often arrived late.

Negative: The witness did not speak during the inquest.

Positive: The witness was silent during the inquest.

Replace:	with:
did not remember	forgot
was not present	was absent
did not pay attention to	ignored

Reserve the negative form for those instances where it produces the desired effect.

> *Of all noises, I think music is the least disagreeable.* — Samuel Johnson

> *I have always been in a condition in which I cannot* not *write.* — Barbara Tuchman

73. Be specific and concrete

Bring abstract ideas down to earth with examples. Help your readers visualize what you're writing about by being specific.

Abstract: The new health and family programs improved employee performance.

Concrete: Absenteeism was reduced by 40% when the company built an employee gym and offered child-care facilities.

Wherever possible, replace abstract words with concrete ones:

Abstract:	Concrete:
vehicle	bicycle
food	steak
color	red
emotion	hatred, confusion

74. Use simple words.

Why write "facilitate his departure" when you can write "help him leave?" Avoid the four- or five-syllable word when one or two syllables convey the idea just as well.

Stilted: Per our aforementioned discussion, I am herewith enclosing a copy of...

Simple: As promised, here is a copy of...

Replace:	with:
utilize	use
ameliorate	improve
modification	change
deficiency	lack
preventative	preventive

75. Avoid overworked words or phrases.

> *Ready-made phrases are the prefabricated strips of words... that come crowding in when you do not want to take the trouble to think through what you are saying... They will construct your sentences for you — even think your thoughts for you, to a certain extent — and at need they will perform the important service of partially concealing your meaning even from yourself.*
> — George Orwell

The saturation provided by television, radio, and the various print media can turn a vogue word into an instant cliché. *Viable, bottom line, parameter, trendy,* and *paradigm* have all joined the catalogue of overworked words. The best way to stifle these word fads is to shun the "in" word or phrase until it has time to recuperate from overuse.

As H.W. Fowler put out in *A Dictionary of Modern English,* hackneyed phrases should be danger signals that the author is writing "bad stuff, or it would not need such help. Let him see to the substance of his cake instead of decorating it with sugarplums."

Fads can be profitable for manufacturers of hula hoops or hot tubs, but word fads profit no one.

76. Eliminate jargon.

In its place, jargon is useful verbal shorthand. Its specialized vocabularies allow members of a particular professional group to communicate succinctly with other members of the group. But jargon has earned its bad reputation because it is often used simply to impress — or worse yet, to provide a smokescreen, burying truth rather than revealing it. Technical language can hide sloppy thinking; fancy words can obscure a lack of understanding or deliberate distortion.

> *It isn't that jargon is noxious in itself, it's that, like crabgrass, the dratted stuff keeps rooting where it doesn't belong.* — Bruce O. Boston

Symptoms of everyday jargon include the following:

a) Interchangeable Parts of Speech

The ability of English to accommodate the crossover of one part of speech into another gives our language some of its liveliness. Nouns become adjectives (milk carton), verbs become nouns (on the mend), and adjectives are used as nouns (seeing red).

The word *author* illustrates the process of change. The 1973 edition of the *Gage Canadian Dictionary* lists *author* as a noun only; the 1983 edition lists it as a verb and a noun.

But too often a satisfactory alternative is ignored and the flexibility of our language is taxed beyond its limits. Careful writers will probably still refrain from using *author* as a verb, and they will certainly avoid such unnecessary shifts in parts of speech as the following.

75

The property was bequested to the school.

Bequeathed or *willed* would be better choices.

Occasionally changing one part of speech into another avoids an awkward construction.

The motion was tabled.

But you can find better ways of saying:

This model obsoletes all its predecessors.

How will that impact on our sales program?

I'll reference that question to the legal staff.

b) Noun chains

When nouns used as adjectives have slipped out of the writer's control, we find such impenetrable chains as the following:

potassium permanganate-impregnated activated alumina medium

or the even more amazing:

multi-million dollar data management peripheral equipment leasing industry.

Brevity was no doubt the motivation behind both of these monstrosities, but when it comes to a face-off between brevity and clarity, clarity should always win. Break up noun chains into manageable portions. For example:

an activated alumina medium that has been impregnated with potassium permanganate or better yet:

> a medium of activated alumina that has been impreg-
> nated with potassium permanganate.

c) Bastard Words

Tacking *-ize* or *-wise* on the end of a legitimate word produces such
illegitimate offspring as *enrollmentwise* and *strategize*. Some *-ize*
words have won respectability (*computerize, idolize, harmonize*);
even the much maligned finalize has some supporters who claim that
alternatives like *complete, conclude, perfect,* or *terminate* do not
carry the meaning of "to put in final form."

Be skeptical about these coined words. Do they accomplish anything? Is an established alternative at hand? Although some are
useful, you avoid branding yourself as a jargoneer if you can find a
satisfactory synonym.

77. Vary sentence length and construction.

Retain reader interest by varying sentence length and by using
different types of sentences. In all contexts other than instructions, a
series of short declarative sentences becomes monotonous. Give your
readers relief from the subject-verb-object order of most sentences
by introducing variety.

Open with a subordinate clause:

> *If any man wishes to write a clear style, let him first be
> clear in his thoughts.* — Johann W. von Goethe

with an infinitive:

> *To get profit without risk, experience without danger,
> and reward without work, is as impossible as it is to live
> without being born.* — A.P. Gouthey

with a participial phrase:

> *Thrusting my nose firmly between his teeth, I threw him heavily to the ground on top of me.* — Mark Twain

with a preposition:

> *Behind the phony tinsel of Hollywood lies the real tinsel.* — Oscar Levant

Notice the rhythm of what you have written — is it choppy, lively, or flowing? Listen to the sound of the words — are there any awkward neighbors like "our products produced..."? Use rhythm, flow, and contrast to make language and meaning harmonious. Try reading out loud what you have written; it can reveal awkward passages and show where punctuation is needed.

78. Watch out for the word *very*.

The word *very* often signals sloppy writing. Overusing it weakens rather than intensifies your meaning.

Poor: His response was very critical.

Better: His response was critical.

Absolutes such as *unique* and *final* stand by themselves; do not attempt to make them more emphatic by adding the word *very*. If *very* seems necessary to strengthen your meaning, consider whether another word that doesn't require such buttressing would be more effective.

Replace:	**with:**
very stubborn	obstinate, bullheaded
very weak	frail, feeble, fragile
very surprised	astonished, astounded, amazed

78

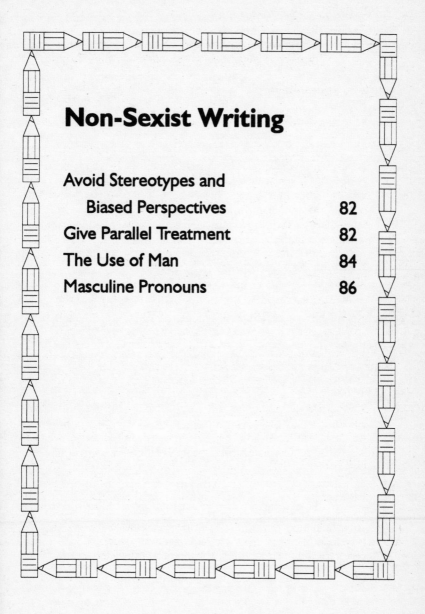

Non-Sexist Writing

NON-SEXIST WRITING

For generations, masculine terms have been used to indicate both sexes. Today, however, you will offend some people if you start a letter with *Dear Sir*, and many female readers will feel excluded if you write "The effective salesman wants his customers to be satisfied." To ignore these sensitivities is unwise, regardless of your views on the subject.

Most writers would agree that it's just plain smart to remove bias from writing. After all, the goal is to communicate, and that's hard to do if your words show prejudice that offends readers. Many writers, however, are unaware of the bias in their writing. Furthermore, this subject is complex and involves issues of length (equal time) and topic (equal presentation) as well as word choice, so most of us need help in avoiding sexist writing.

It is surprisingly easy to avoid sexist terms — simply acknowledging the problem is an important first step. You do not have to use language that is awkward or silly to avoid offending your readers. But using a good substitute for *chairman* or *Gentlemen* improves the likelihood of your having a sympathetic audience.

A detailed exploration of sexist terms and their social implications is beyond the scope of this book. The topic has been thoroughly covered by Casey Miller and Kate Swift in their book *The Handbook of Non-sexist Writing* (Lippincott & Crowell, 1980). The goal here is to review some of the alternatives currently being adopted.

The following pages suggest ways to avoid trouble spots in your writing. As you develop new habits, you may find that non-sexist writing is actually better writing.

79. Avoid stereotypes and biased perspectives

Your attitudes and biases can easily creep into your writing through stereotypes and skewed perspectives if you are not careful. For example:

Biased: The company picnic will be open to all employees, their wives, and families.

Biased: The discreet secretary never discusses her boss's business with his staff.

Biased: *True patriot love in all thy sons command.* — O Canada!

The first sentence assumes that all employees are men; the second implies that all secretaries are female and all bosses, male. The last sentence seems to dismiss all patriotic "daughters" of the nation.

These sentences could be rewritten:

Neutral: The company picnic will be open to all employees, their spouses, and families.

Neutral: The discreet secretary never discusses the boss's business with staff members.

Neutral: True patriot love in everyone command.

80. Give parallel treatment

Don't mention the sex of a person unless it is pertinent.

Biased: Margaret Bourke-White was a woman photographer who gained worldwide recognition.

Neutral: Margaret Bourke-White was a photographer who gained worldwide recognition.

Do not describe a woman's physical appearance where you would have described a man's professional qualifications:

Biased: Ed Reed, a distinguished attorney with a long record of community service, and his partner Diane Wells, an elegantly dressed, statuesque black woman, entered the courtroom.

Neutral: Ed Reed and Diane Wells are distinguished attorneys who have served as unpaid advocates in their communities.

Use comparable language when identifying individuals. A columnist in a national magazine failed to do so when he described the activities in a packing room:

> A young man planed and sanded the wood...A girl was fitting a sculpture into a specially made crate.

If she is a "girl," then he should be a "boy." Or the writer could have elevated her to the status of a "young woman."

> After dinner, the ladies retired to the drawing room while the men remained at the table for port and cigars.

Either the "women retired" and the "men remained" or the "ladies retired" and the "gentlemen remained."

Uneven	Even
ladies and men	women and men
Roger Evans and Mrs. Platt	Roger Evans and Donna Platt
Mr. Evans and Donna	Mr. Evans and Ms. Platt

81. The use of *man*

Whether as a prefix *(manpower)*, a suffix *(chairman)*, or a word by itself, *man* evokes a strong reaction from some readers. Many women feel that using *man* as a word for people of both sexes when it is also clearly associated with adult males relegates women to a second-class status. You may not share this view; there is considerable precedent for using *man* to mean all human beings. But that will bring little consolation if insisting on using the term in this general sense muddies your meaning or alienates your reader. There are other ways to express the concept. Here are some examples:

alderman	councillor
anchorman	anchor
ancient man	our ancestors
businessman	executive, manager, merchant
chairman	chair
common man	average person
draftsman	drafter
foreman	supervisor
layman	layperson
longshoreman	dock worker
mailman	letter carrier
man (noun)	human, human beings, persons, human race
man (verb)	staff (as in *staff the booth*), operate, run
manmade	artificial, synthetic, handmade
manpower	personnel, staff, workers
newsman	reporter, journalist
salesman	sales rep, salesperson
repairman	service rep

Note that words like *chairman* and *businessman* are perfectly appropriate when used in conjunction with a specific male and if you would use *chairwoman* and *businesswoman* when referring to their female counterparts. Be careful you don't end up calling the male *chairman* and the female *chairperson*; that is not parallel writing.

The following sentences illustrate some common uses of *man* and suggest alternative wordings.

Biased: All men are created equal.

Neutral: All people are created equal.
(Unless you mean to refer only to adult males.)

Biased: Ancient man devised ways to observe the motions of the planets.

Neutral: Our ancestors devised ways to observe the motions of the planets.

Biased: Unemployment rates are meaningful to the average working man whose job may be on the line.

Neutral: Unemployment rates are meaningful to the average worker whose job may be on the line.

Biased: Pollsters rely on the opinion of the man in the street for their predictions.

Neutral: Pollsters rely on the opinion of the average person for their predictions.

A common misunderstanding is that we should avoid the syllable *man* wherever it occurs. This confusion created a national pastime as we dreamed up outrageous substitutes such as *personhole* and *personeuver*.

But the syllable *man* does not always derive from the word *man*. Words such as *manipulate, manage,* and *manuscript* are derived from the Latin *manus* (hand); they have no roots in common with our word *man* and present no problems of ambiguity. There is no need to substitute other terms for the syllable *man*.

82. Masculine pronouns

It would be convenient if we had a singular word as neutral as *they* to substitute for the masculine pronouns *he, him,* and *his* when referring to females as well as males. Unfortunately, we do not, and this has led to sentences such as:

> Every man and woman must find his own way to spiritual peace so that he can exist in harmony with his world.

Some writers attempt to avoid this problem by using the plural pronouns *they* and *their*:

> Every man and woman must find their own way to spiritual peace so that they can exist in harmony with their world.

This is, however, grammatically incorrect. Fortunately, there are other, better ways to eliminate inappropriate male pronouns, including —

(a) changing the subject from singular to plural,
(b) using both pronouns,
(c) writing in the second person,
(d) repeating the noun, and
(e) revising the sentence.

a) Change from singular to plural

If you can change the subject from a singular to a plural, you are then free to use the neutral plural pronouns *they, their,* and *them.*

Biased: *Since a politician never believes what he says, he is always astonished when others do.* — Charles DeGaulle

Neutral: Since politicians never believe what they say, they are are always astonished when others do.

Biased: *I can remember way back when a liberal was one who was generous with his own money.* — Will Rogers

Neutral: I can remember way back when liberals were the ones who were generous with their own money.

b) Use both pronouns

If the plural form is not appropriate, you may prefer to write *he or she, her or his,* or *him or her.*

> The director told the actors that everyone should show up for the next rehearsal wearing his or her costume.

In occasional use, the awkwardness of this construction is probably not a serious drawback, but repeated use suggests that you should rewrite to avoid these pronouns altogether:

Poor: Every man and woman must find his or her own way to spiritual peace so that he or she can exist in harmony with his or her world.

Better: Every man and woman must find a way to spiritual peace in order to exist in harmony with the world.

c) Write in the second person

In some circumstances, you can address the reader as *you* (second person) rather than as the more anonymous *he* or *she*. This is particularly true of instructions.

Change: Anyone wishing to receive a free subscription should enclose payment with his order.

to: If you wish to receive a free subscription, enclose payment with your order.

Change: Every man and woman must find his own way to spiritual peace so that he can exist in harmony with his world.

to: You must find your own way to spiritual peace so that you can exist in harmony with your world.

d) Repeat the noun

For the sake of simple clarity, it is often better to repeat the noun than to use an imprecise pronoun.

Change: The homeowner who employs a gardener should ensure that he owns the necessary tools.

to: The homeowner who employs a gardener should ensure that the gardener owns the necessary tools.

The first sentence is not only sexist, it is imprecise, as it is difficult to determine who should own the tools.

e) Revise the sentence

This is frequently the best solution to getting bogged down with pronouns. The variety of ways we can express ourselves makes rewriting a relatively simple matter.

Revise: The tennis player must practice his serve.

to: The tennis player must practice serving.

Revise: The child who is afraid to go to bed by himself.

to: The child who is afraid to go to bed alone.

Confused and Abused Words

advice/advise
affect/effect
allude/refer
allusion/illusion
alright
alternate/alternate
ante/anti
bad/badly
can/may
capital/capitol
complement/compliment
comprise
contact
continual/continuous
council/counsel/consul
different from/different than
discreet/discrete
disinterested/uninterested
ecology
emigrate/immigrate
eminent/imminent
enthuse

farther/further
fewer/less
flammable/inflammable
flaunt/flaut
foreword/forward
hopefully
I/me/myself
imply/infer
insure/ensure/assure
irregardless
it's/its
lay/lie
lend/loan
like/as
loose/lose
meantime/meanwhile
people/persons
predominant/predominate
principal/principle
shall/will
stationary/stationery
that/which
that/adverbial
that/who/whose
was/were
who/whom

CONFUSED AND ABUSED WORDS

The difference between the right word and the almost right word is the difference between lightning and the lightning bug. — Mark Twain

The following list may help you tell the difference.

Advice/Advise: The noun *advice* means suggestion or counsel; the verb *advise* means to give advice.

> I advise you not to take her advice.

Affect/Effect: Perhaps the easiest way to sort out the confusion about these two words is to remember that the most common use of *affect* is as a verb, and of *effect* is as a noun.

The verb *affect* means to influence or to produce an effect on.

> The lawyer hoped to affect the jury's decision.

A less common meaning of *affect* as a verb is to pretend, to simulate, or imitate in order to make some desired impression.

> The lawyer affected a look of disbelief when the defendant was unable to recall his whereabouts.

The noun *effect* means result of consequence.

> The lawyer's closing statement had an effect on the jury.

The verb *effect* means to bring about.

> The new manager effected many changes in personnel.

Chances are that if the sentence calls for a verb, affect is the word you want; if the sentence calls for a noun, effect is the appropriate word.

Allude/Refer: To *allude* to something is to mention it indirectly, without identifying it specifically. To *refer* is to indicate directly.

> The speaker alluded to the hazards of obesity when he referred to the chart showing life expectancy and weight.

Allusion/Illusion: *Allusion,* the noun form of the verb *allude,* means an indirect reference to something not specifically identified, while *illusion* is a mistaken perception.

Alright: Common misspelling of the words *all right.*

Alternate/Alternative: *Alternate* refers to every other one, or following by turns; *alternative* is a choice.

Ante/Anti: *Ante-* means before or in front of. *Anti-* means against.

> The people in the anteroom are all anti-nuclear protesters.

Bad/badly: To help you tell whether to use the adjective *bad* or the adverb *badly*, substitute a synonym in a sentence that calls for one or the other.

> I feel (*bad, badly*) about the incident.

Substitute *unhappy* and *unhappily.* Which fits? Clearly, you wouldn't write "I feel unhappily…"; just so, you shouldn't write "I feel badly about the incident."

Bi/Semi: You won't find 100% agreement among experts, but most favor the use of *bi-,* as in *bimonthly* or *biweekly,* to mean every two months or weeks. The prefix *semi-* is reserved for the meaning of half or occurring twice within the time period. Thus, a bimonthly meeting would take place every two months, and a semimonthly meeting would occur twice each month. An exception is biannual, which means twice a year; biennial means every two years.

Can/May: Written usage requires that you distinguish between *can* and *may*; *can* means ability or power to do something, *may* means permission to do it.

You may have dessert if you can eat your vegetables.

Capital/Capitol: *Capital* refers to wealth, the city that is the seat of government, or an upper case letter. *Capitol* is the building in which government officials congregate, and it is used most frequently in the United States. The *Capitol,* when referring to the home of the U.S. Congress, is always capitalized.

The Prime Minister will visit U.S. senators at the Capitol.

Complement/Compliment: *Complement* is both a verb and a noun, meaning to complete a whole or satisfy a need. *Compliment* means praise and also functions as both verb and noun.

His efforts complemented those of the rest of the team. (verb)

A complement of 12 soldiers performed the assignment. (noun)

She complimented him on the apple pie he had baked. (verb)

Her compliment was sincere. (noun)

Nowadays we are all of us so hard up that the only pleasant things to pay are compliments. — Oscar Wilde

Comprise: One of our most abused words, *comprise* means to include or be made up of; it is frequently confused with *compose* or incorrectly used as a synonym for *constitute.* The whole comprises the parts; the parts constitute the whole.

Wrong: High tech comprises only 6% of GNP.

Right: High tech constitutes only 6% of GNP.

Right: The company comprises three divisions.

Contact: Widely accepted as a noun that has successfully made the transition into a verb, *contact* is nonetheless an overworked word.

93

Avoid using it when a satisfactory synonym is available, such as *phone, write,* or *reach.*

Continual/Continuous: *Continual* means over and over again, whereas *continuous* should only be used to mean uninterrupted or unbroken.

> Since he coughed continually, the doctor kept him under continuous observation.

> *A man's memory may almost become the art of continually varying and misrepresenting his past, according to his interests in the present.* — George Santayana

Council/Counsel/Consul: *Council,* always a noun, refers to an assemblage of persons or a committee. *Counsel* has both verb and noun forms, meaning to advise, the advice itself, or an attorney.

> Counsel for the defense counselled the defense not to speak to the council members; the council resented his counsel.

Consul is a person in the foreign service of a country.

Different from/Different than: *Different from* is preferred when it is followed by a noun or short phrase.

> His writing style is different from mine.

Different than is acceptable when its use avoids wordiness or when different is followed by a clause.

> Today the concept of women's rights is different than it was at the turn of the century.

Discreet/Discrete: *Discreet* is used to describe behavior that is prudent or respectful of propriety. *Discrete* frequently has a scientific connotation and means separate, distinct, or individual.

> He made discreet inquiries into her whereabouts.

The smooth surface of water seems to contradict the discrete nature of its molecules.

Disinterested/Uninterested: *Disinterested* should only be used to convey objectivity or neutrality, while *uninterested* is simply lacking interest.

A disinterested scientist would not necessarily be uninterested in the results of the experiment.

Ecology: The study of the relationship between organisms and their environment. Often misused as a synonym for *environment.*

Emigrate/Immigrate: To *emigrate* is to leave one's country permanently, thus one emigrates *from* a country. To *immigrate* is to move to a new country permanently, thus one immigrates *to* a country.

Eminent/Imminent: *Eminent* means well known or distinguished, while *imminent* means about to happen.

The arrival of the eminent statesman was imminent.

Enthuse: An informal form of the word *enthusiastic* that is not acceptable in formal writing. Rewrite to avoid its use.

Farther/Further: *Farther* should be reserved for ideas of physical distance. Use *further* in all other senses, specifically when indicating additional time, degree, or quantity.

We walked farther than we had intended.

The jury expressed the need for further deliberation.

The distinction between these two words will probably disappear eventually; as Theodore Bernstein points out in *The Careful Writer,* "It looks as if farther is going to be mowed down by the scythe of Old Further Time."

Fewer/Less: Generally, *less* is used for quantity, *fewer* for number.

Fewer potatoes, less mush.

Fewer is preferred when referring to individual numbers or units, while *less* is used in sentences involving periods of time, sums of money, or measures of distance and weight.

> Automation requires more machines and fewer people.

> He ran the mile in less than four minutes.

Flammable/Inflammable: Both mean capable of burning.

Flaunt/Flout: A common error is to use *flaunt,* which means to show off, for *flout,* which means to show contempt. Although sometimes widespread errors evolve into acceptability, confusing these two words is simply an error.

Foreword/Forward: *Foreword* is a preface or introductory note. Notice the spelling: It deals with words and is spelled with an *o.* *Forward* means the opposite of backward. There is no such word as *foreward.*

Hopefully: Means with hope, in a hopeful manner. Frequently — and incorrectly — used with the meaning of "it is to be hoped" or "I hope."

I/Me/Myself: *I* is the subjective case and thus should be used when it is the subject of the sentence (the *who* or *what* that the rest of the sentence is about):

> My brother and I went to the ball game.

Me is the objective case and should be used when it is the object of the action or thought conveyed by the verb of the sentence, or is the object of a preposition:

> Between you and me, I hate Sunday afternoon football games.

> Stan invited Mark and me to a beach party.

In a sentence like the last, if you remove "Mark and," it quickly becomes obvious that me is the correct pronoun.

Myself is used for emphasis:

> I'd rather do it myself.

or as a reflexive pronoun (i.e., turning the action back on the grammatical subject):

> I was able to feed myself when I was very young.

It is incorrect to use *myself* as a substitute for *I* or *me*.

Wrong: The gift was presented to both my brother and myself.

Right: The gift was presented to both my brother and me.

Wrong: My partner and myself have entered into a new agreement.

Right: My partner and I have entered into a new agreement.

Imply/Infer: To *imply* is to suggest indirectly or insinuate; to *infer* is to draw a conclusion or deduce. Generally, a speaker implies and listeners infer.

Insure/Ensure/Assure: All three words mean to make secure or certain.

> Victory is assured (or ensured or insured).

Assure has the meaning of setting someone's mind at rest. Both *ensure* and *insure* mean to make secure from harm. Only *insure* should be used regarding guaranteeing of life or property against risk.

Irregardless: A redundancy. Use *regardless*.

It's/Its: *It's* is the contraction of *it is*. *Its* is a possessive pronoun.

Lay/Lie: *Lay* is a transitive verb (i.e., it takes an object) meaning to place or put down.

Lay the package on the table. (*Package* is the object of the verb *lay.*)

Lie is an intransitive verb (i.e., it does not take an object) meaning to recline.

Lie on your exercise mat.

Lend/Loan: *Lend* is a verb, and *loan* is primarily a noun. However, the use of *loan* as a verb seems to be more and more prevalent, and it completely dominates business circles. If the past tense of *lend* sounds awkward, use *loan.*

She loaned the museum three paintings.

The bank loaned the company $100,000.

But wherever possible, hold the line on abuses of the word. For instance, say "Lend me your pen," not "Loan me your pen."

Like/As: *Like* is correct when it functions as a preposition.

She sang like an angel.

My Luv is like a red, red rose. — Robert Burns

Like is also acceptable when it introduces a clause in which the verb has been omitted.

She took to politics like a fish to water.

As should be used instead of like when the clause includes a verb.

She took to politics as a fish takes to water.

Like as a conjunction is generally unacceptable and should be replaced by *as, as if,* or *as though.*

Truffles taste good, as an epicurean dish should.

We can act as if there were a God; feel as if we were free; consider Nature as if she were full of special designs; lay plans as if we were to be immortal; and we find then that these words do make a genuine difference in our moral life. — William James

Loose/Lose: *Loose* is an adjective meaning unrestrained or not fastened. *Lose* is a verb meaning the opposite of win or the opposite of find.

Meantime/Meanwhile: Meantime is usually a noun describing the interval between one event and other; meanwhile is an adverb meaning during or in the intervening time.

> In the meantime, back at the ranch…

> Meanwhile, back at the ranch…

In the meantime and *meanwhile* can usually be interchanged. But do not say *in the meanwhile.*

People/Persons: In general, use *people* for large groups, persons for an exact or small number.

> Eight persons are being held as hostages.

> *Hell is — other people!* — Jean Paul Sartre

Predominant/Predominate: *Predominant* is an adjective meaning most common, or having the greatest influence or force. *Predominate* is a verb meaning to have the greatest influence, to prevail.

> The predominant theme of the event was patriotism.

> The patriotic theme of the event predominated over all others.

Principal/Principle: *Principal* functions as both noun and adjective. The noun refers to the head of a school or firm, or to capital which earns interest; the adjective means chief or main. *Principle* is a noun meaning rule or standard.

99

The principal's principal principle was *Do Thy Homework.*

Women without principle draw considerable interest.

Shall/Will: This is one instance where fading of an old grammatical distinction has left us none the poorer. Don't worry about rules regarding *shall* and *will* — just let your ear be your guide. *Shall* is frequently used to express determination.

> *I shall return.* — Douglas MacArthur

Stationary/Stationery: *Stationary* means fixed in one place, not moving. *Stationery* is writing envelopes. A good way to remember is that *stationery* is what you need to write letters.

That/Which: The *that/which* problem takes up six pages in Fowler's *Dictionary of Modern English Usage.* For most people, it is sufficient to distinguish between the two relative pronouns by using *that* to introduce a restrictive clause (one that is essential to the meaning):

> The river that flows by our house is at a low level.

> *Beware of all enterprises that require new clothes.* — Thoreau

and by using *which* to introduce a nonrestrictive or parenthetical clause:

> The river, which overflows its banks every year, is now at a low level.

That (adverbial): In the sense of "to that degree or amount," *that* is standard usage (I won't buy a car that old). But "I am not that hungry" is considered informal usage, unless it is preceded by something like "John ate 12 pancakes." If readers have nothing to refer to, they are left wondering how hungry "that hungry" is.

That/Who/Whose: The rule requiring the use of *that* when referring to things and *who* when referring to persons has been relaxed. Now you may choose whichever word seems more natural when referring to either persons or things.

The most impartial judge that could be found...

Anyone who can answer my question...

That building, whose architect is a local resident...

The fellow that owns his own home is always just com-
ing out of a hardware store. — Kin Hubbard

Was/Were: When expressing a wish or a condition contrary to fact,
and following the words *as if* and *as though,* use *were:*

The silence made it seem as if he were speaking to an
empty room.

If it were not for the presents, an elopement would be
preferable. — George Ade

In expressing a past condition not contrary to fact, use *was:*

If Deborah was guilty, she did not show it.

Who/Whom: The best guide for deciding which of these words to
use is to substitute a personal pronoun in place of a word; if *he, she,*
or *they* would fit, use *who* (nominative case); if *him, her,* or *them*
would fit, use *whom* (objective case).

This is the man who you thought committed the crime.
(you thought *he* committed the crime)

To whom shall I report? (to *him, her,* or *them*)

Champlain, whom we all read about in school... (we
read about *him*)

Margaret Laurence, who wrote the book... (*she* wrote)

For prying into any human affairs, none are equal to those whom it does not concern. — Victor Hugo (it does not concern *them*)

The best liar is he who makes the smallest amount of lying go the longest way. — Samuel Butler (*he* makes the smallest amount)

The multitude, who require to be led, still hate their leaders. — William Hazlitt (*they* require to be led)

Venolia's Reverse Rules
for Writers

VENOLIA'S REVERSE RULES FOR WRITERS

Sometimes a tongue-in-cheek approach is effective in fixing a subject in our minds. In that spirit, I present the following summary of the subjects covered in *Write Right!* — plus a few not mentioned.

1. Put the apostrophe where its needed.

2. Never let a colon separate: the main parts of the sentence.

3. Avoid overuse, of commas.

4. Reserve the dash — which is — often — overused — for emphasis.

5. Avoid un-necessary hyphens; divide words only between syllables.

6. Use a semicolon where needed, use it properly; and never where not called for.

7. Avoid run-on sentences they seem to go on forever.

8. In general, don't abbrev.

9. Have a good reason for Capitalizing a word.

10. In formal writing, don't use contractions.

11. Consult a dictionery for correct spelling.

12. Observe the rule that verbs has to agree with their subjects.

13. Make each subject and pronoun agree in their number, too.

14. Use parallel construction in writing sentences, forming paragraphs, and to emphasize a point.

15. After studying these rules, dangling modifiers will be easy to correct.

16. Omit unnecessary, excess words that aren't needed.

17. Generally, writing should be in the active voice.

18. Don't use trendy words whose parameters are not viable.

19. Avoid verbing a noun.

20. The careful writer avoids bias in his words.

21. Watch out for irregular verbs that have crope into your language.

22. Eschew archaic words.

23. Proof carefully in case you nay words out.

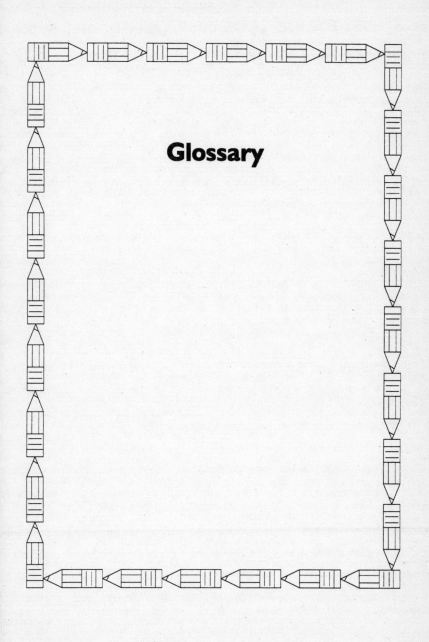

Glossary

GLOSSARY

Active Voice: The form of the verb used when the subject performs the action. See Rule 71.

Adjective: Modifies (describes or limits) a noun or pronoun. It may be a single word, phrase, or clause. See Parts of Speech.

> *As to the adjective: when in doubt, strike it out.*
> — Mark Twain

Adverb: Modifies a verb, an adjective, or another adverb. May be a single word, phrase, or clause. See Parts of Speech.

Antecedent: The word, phrase, or clause referred to by a pronoun.

> *Everyone has talent. What is rare is the courage to follow the talent to the dark place where it leads.*
> — Erica Jong

Antonym: A word having a meaning opposite to that of another word.

spicy/bland   ill/healthy

Appositive: A word, phrase, or clause placed near a noun to explain it and having the same grammatical relation to the rest of the sentence as the word it describes.

> My son, *the doctor,* sends me a card every
> Mother's Day.

Article: The words *a, an,* and *the.*

Case: The means by which the relationship of a noun or pronoun to the rest of the sentence is shown. There are three cases: nominative (also known as subjective), objective, and possessive.

Nominative: the case of the subject of the verb.

> *We* entered the room.

Objective: the case of the object of a verb or preposition.

> He threw the *ball* to *me*.

(*Ball* is the object of the verb *threw; me* is the object of the preposition *to*.)

Possessive: the case that shows ownership.

> Here is *your* answer.

> Take away the *dog's* bone.

Clause: A group of words that contains a subject and verb.

Co-ordinate clauses have the same rank and are connected by a co-ordinating conjunction.

> It started to rain, so we left the football game.

Dependent clauses (also known as subordinate) do not make sense when standing alone.

> *He watches the late news* before he goes to bed.

Independent clauses (also called principal or main) are those which would make complete sense if left standing alone.

> *He watches the late news* before going to bed.

Nonrestrictive clauses could be omitted without changing the meaning; they are surrounded by commas.

> Sylvia, *who reads a great deal,* has a large vocabulary.

Restrictive clauses are essential to the meaning (i.e., could not be left out without changing the meaning of the sentence).

> People *who read a great deal* have large vocabularies.

> *There are few chaste women who are not tired of their trade.* — LaRochefoucauld

Comma Fault: The error in which a comma is used as the sole connection between two independent clauses.

Wrong: The company picnic is an annual event, this year it will be held at the beach.

The above sentence would be correct if a conjunction such as *and* were added or the comma replaced with a semicolon or period.

Complement: A word or phrase that completes the meaning of the verb.

> *Great artists need <u>great clients</u>.* — I.M. Pei

> *I owe <u>the public nothing</u>.* — J.P. Morgan

> *Information is the <u>currency of democracy</u>.* — Ralph Nader

Compound: Consisting of two or more elements.

A *compound adjective,* also known as a unit modifier, consists of two or more adjectives modifying the same noun.

> *I'm a tall, gangly, high-bred Canadian who won't be pushed around.* — Susan Clark

A *compound sentence* consists of two or more independent clauses.

> *Balloonists have an unsurpassed view of the scenery, but there is always the possibility that it may collide with them.* — H.L. Mencken

A *compound subject* consists of two or more subjects having the same verb.

> *Papa, potatoes, poultry, prunes, and prism are all very good words for the lips: especially prunes and prism.* — Charles Dickens

A *compound verb* consists of two or more verbs having the same subject.

> *We are born crying, live complaining, and die disappointed.* — Thomas Fuller

Conjunction: A single word or group of words that connects other words or groups of words. See Parts of Speech.

Co-ordinate conjunctions connect words, phrases, or clauses of equal rank; for example, *and, but, or, nor, for, however, moreover, then, therefore, yet, still, both/and, not only/but also, either/or, neither/nor.*

Subordinate conjunctions connect clauses of unequal rank (i.e., an independent and dependent clause). Examples are *as, as if, because, before, if, since, that, till, unless, when, where, whether.*

Dangling Modifier: A modifier with an unclear reference. See Rule 69.

Gerund: The *-ing* form of a verb that serves as a noun.

> *Seeing* is *believing.*

> Does anyone object to my *smoking*?

(Note the possessive pronoun; "Does anyone object to *me* smoking?" would be incorrect.)

Idiom: Idiomatic expressions, such as *rubbing someone the wrong way,* do not conform to the logic of a language. Either the meaning of the expression cannot be derived from the meaning of the individual words (*to take in, to make up for*), or their construction violates grammatical rules (*Take it easy,* not *Take it easily*).

Infinitive: The form of a verb used with *to.*

> *I don't want <u>to achieve</u> immortality through my work. I want <u>to achieve</u> it through not dying.* — Woody Allen

Intransitive Verb: A verb that does not require an object to complete its meaning. A given verb can be either transitive (i.e., requiring an object) or intransitive, depending on its use.

> He met his sister at the airport. (Transitive - *sister* is the object of the verb *met*).

> The delegates met last week. (Intransitive - no object)

Misplaced Modifier: A modifier that gives a misleading meaning by being incorrectly placed in a sentence. See Rule 68.

Nonrestrictive Elements: Words, phrases, or clauses that are not essential to the meaning.

Noun: A word that names a person, place, thing, quality, or act. See Parts of Speech.

A *proper noun* names a specific person, place, or thing; it is capitalized.

> the Big Apple, Julius Caesar, Hallowe'en

Number: Changes made, such as adding an *s,* to reflect whether a word is singular or plural.

> **Singular:** a porcupine

> **Plural:** three porcupines

Object: The word or phrase that names the thing acted upon by the subject and verb. Objects are complements; they complete the meaning of the verb.

She visited *the ancient cathedral.*

A *direct object* names the thing acted upon by the subject.

I bought a *book.*

An *indirect object* receives whatever is named by the direct object.

Participle: A form of a verb which has some of the properties of an adjective and some of a verb. Like an adjective, it can modify a noun or pronoun; like a verb, it can take an object.

Success is <u>getting</u> what you want; happiness is <u>wanting</u> what you get.

Glowing coals, *frayed* collars, *run-down* heels, and *whipped* cream are examples of verb forms that function as adjectives, and thus are participles.

Parts of Speech: Nouns, pronouns, verbs, adjectives, adverbs, prepositions, conjunctions, and interjections. In the days of *McGuffey's Reader,* students used to learn the parts of speech with the help of the following jingle:

A NOUN's the name of anything,
As, *school* or *garden, hoop* or *swing.*

ADJECTIVES tell the kind of noun;
As, *great, small, pretty, white,* or *brown.*

Instead of nouns the PRONOUNS stand:
Their heads, *your* face, *its* paw, *his* hand.

VERBS tell of something being done:
You *read, count, sing, laugh, jump,* or *run.*

How things are done the ADVERBS tell;
As, *slowly, quickly, ill,* or *well.*

CONJUNCTIONS join the words together;
As, men *and* women, wind *or* weather.

The PREPOSITION stands before
a noun; as, *in* or *through* a door.

The INTERJECTION shows surprise;
As, *Oh!* how pretty! *Ah!* how wise!

Passive Voice: The form of the verb used when the subject is the receiver of the action. See Rule 71.

Person: Person denotes the speaker (first person), the person spoken to (second person), or the person or thing spoken of (third person).

Possessive: Showing ownership; also known as the genitive case. See Case.

> *He is a sheep in <u>sheep's</u> clothing.* — Winston Churchill

Predicate: A group of words that makes a statement or asks a question about the subject of a sentence. A *simple predicate* consists of a verb (*can preach,* in the following example). A *complete predicate* includes verbs, modifiers, objects, and complements (*can preach a better sermon with your life than with your lips*).

> *You can preach a better sermon with your life than with your lips.* — Oliver Goldsmith

Prefix: A word element which is attached to the front of a root word and changes the meaning of the root: *dis*belief, *in*attentive.

Preposition: A word or group of words that shows the relation between its object and some other word in the sentence. See Parts of Speech.

> *The murals in restaurants are <u>on</u> a par <u>with</u> the food <u>in</u> museums.* — Peter DeVries

Perhaps no other rule of grammar has prompted so many to say so much as the now-outdated rule prohibiting ending a sentence with a preposition. Here are two comments on the subject:

> *This is the sort of English up with which I will not put.*
> — Winston Churchill

> *The grammar has a rule absurd*
> *Which I would call an outworn myth:*
> *A preposition is a word*
> *You mustn't end a sentence with.* — Berton Braley

Pronoun: A word that takes the place of a noun. See Parts of Speech.

Possessive pronouns represent the possessor and the thing possessed:

> The book is *mine*.

Personal pronouns are *I, you, he, she, it,* and their inflected forms (*me, my, your, them,* etc.).

Relative pronouns (who, which, that, what) join adjective clauses to their antecedents (i.e., what they refer to):

> The girl *who* sang is here.

Restrictive Elements: Words, phrases, or clauses that are essential to the meaning.

> The tennis match ended in a tie everyone agreed that it was too late to play a tie-breaker.

This error would be corrected by any of the following: adding a semicolon between the two clauses; making the clauses into separate sentences; or adding a comma and a conjunction between the clauses.

> The tennis match ended in a tie; everyone agreed that it was too late to play a tie-breaker.

> The tennis match ended in a tie. Everyone agreed that it was too late to play a tie-breaker.

The tennis match ended in a tie, but everyone agreed that it was too late to play a tie-breaker.

Sentence: A combination of words that contains at least one subject and predicate (grammatical definition); a group of words that expresses a complete thought (popular definition).

A *simple sentence* consists of subject and predicate; in other words, an independent clause.

> *Our sense of identity is our sense of density.* —
> Marshall McLuhan

A *compound sentence* consists of two or more independent clauses.

> *Life is a shipwreck, but we must not forget to sing in the lifeboats.* — Voltaire

A *complex sentence* consists of one independent clause and one or more dependent (subordinate) clauses; in the following example, the independent clause is underlined.

> <u>*New York is the only city in the world*</u> *where you can be deliberately run down on the sidewalk by a pedestrian.*
> — Russell Baker

Subject: The part of a sentence about which something is said.

> *Time* flies.

Subjective Case: Nominative case. See Case.

Subordinate Clause: See Clause, Dependent.

Suffix: A word element added to the end of a root or stem word, serving to make a new word or an inflected form of a word: gentle*ness*, mother*hood*, depend*able*, hilar*ious*, end*ed*, child*ren*, walk*ing*.

Transitive Verb: A verb that requires a direct object to complete its meaning. See Intransitive Verb.

Unit Modifier: See Compound Adjective.

Verb: A word that expresses action, being, or occurrence. See Parts of Speech.

Voice: See Active Voice, Passive Voice.

Frequently Misspelled Words

FREQUENTLY MISSPELLED WORDS*

Note: The following list contains several pairs of "sound-alikes." A brief definition identifies the first of the sound-alike words; the second is defined following its alphabetical entry.

A

abacus
aberration
abridgment
abscess
abscissa
absence
accelerator
accept (receive)
  except
accessible
accessory
accommodate
accumulate
achievement
acknowledgment
acquittal
acumen
acupuncture
adjourn
adolescence
advantageous
advertisement
aegis

aerosol
affidavit
aging
algae
algorithm
align
alimony
alkaline
allegiance
allotment
allotted
all right
already
amanuensis
amoeba
amplifier
anachronism
analogous
analysis
ancillary
anesthetic
annihilate
anomaly
anonymous

antihistamine
apartheid
aperture
aphrodisiac
apparatus
apparel
apparent
appraisal
apropos
aqueduct
arctic
arraign
arteriosclerosis
arthritis
ascorbic
asphyxiate
aspirin
assessor
assistance
asterisk
asymmetry
attendance
attorneys
auditor

*In Canada, the spelling of many words is optional. The use of *our* in words like *colour* and *honour* is gradually giving way to *or,* as you will notice in almost every newspaper. Where two spellings are given here, the first one seems to be the more widely used one now, although both are acceptable.

autumn
auxiliary

B

bachelor
bailiff
balance
ballistic
balloon
ballot
bankruptcy
barbiturate
barrel
basically
beneficiary
benign
bereave
berserk
bifurcate
bigot
bilateral
bilingual
binary
biodegradable
biopsy
bipartisan
blatant
bloc (group)
bludgeon
bologna
bouillon (soup)
  bullion
bourgeois
boutique
boycott
braille
brief

bruise
budget
bulletin
bullion (gold)
  bouillon
bureaucracy
burglar
business
byte

C

caffeine
calendar
calorie
campaign
cannot
capillary
capitulate
capsule
captain
carafe
carat
carbohydrate
carburetor
Caribbean
carriage
catechism
category
cathode
Caucasian
caucus
caveat
ceiling
cellar
cellophane
Celsius
cemetery

censor
centigrade
centimetre,
  centimeter
centrifugal
cerebral
certain
cesarean
  (or Caesarean)
chaise longue
champagne
changeable
charisma
chassis
chauvinist
chiropractor
chlorophyll
chocolate
cholesterol
Christian
cipher
circuit
cirrhosis
clone
clothes
coalition
cocaine
coefficient
cognac
coliseum
  (or colosseum)
collar
collateral
colloquial
cologne
colonel
color, colour

colossal
column
commitment
commodities
compatible
competent
computer
condemn
conductor
conduit
conglomerate
conjugal
conscience
consensus
consortium
corps
correspondence
counterfeit
coup d'etat
courtesy
cousin
cryptic
cul-de-sac
culinary
curtain
cybernetics
cylinder

D

database
debit
debugging
decadence
deceive
decibel

deciduous
deductible
defendant
defence, defense
deferred
deficit
depot
depreciate
descend
desiccate
desperate
deterrent
develop
diagnostic
diaphragm
dichotomy
dictionary
diesel
digital
dilemma
dinosaur
director
disappear
disappoint
disburse (pay out)
 disperse
discernible
discreet (cautious)
discrete (separate)
disperse (scatter)
 disburse
dissatisfied
dissipate
distributor
doubt

dyeing (coloring)
dying (death)

E

eccentric
echelon
ecstasy
eighth
either
elevator
elicit (draw forth)
 illicit
embarrass
emphysema
empirical
encyclopedia
endeavor,
 endeavour
entrepreneur
envelop (surround)
envelope
 (stationery)
epitome
equipped
equity
equivocal
errata
erratic
erroneous
esoteric
esthetic
 (or aesthetic)
euthanasia
exaggerate

except (other than)
  accept
exhaust
exhibition
exhilarate
existential
exonerate
exorbitant
exponential
extraterrestrial

F

facsimile
factor
Fahrenheit
fallacy
familiar
favor, favour
faze (disturb)
  phase
feasibility
feature
February
fetus
fiduciary
fierce
filibuster
finesse
fission
fluorescent
fluoridate
focused
  (or focussed)
foreign
foreword
forfeit

franchise
freight
fulfill

G

galaxy
gallon
garrulous
genealogy
generic
geriatrics
gestalt
ghetto
governor
graffiti
gram
grammar
grateful
grief
grievance
guarantee
guerilla
  or guerrilla
guess
gynecology

H

hallucinogen
handkerchief
harass
Hawaiian
height
heinous
heir
hemorrhage
herbicide
heroin (drug)

hertz
hiatus
hierarchy
hirsute
holistic
holocaust
hologram
homogeneous
homonym
honor, honour
hors d'oeuvres
hospice
hydraulic
hygiene
hymn
hypnosis
hypocrisy

I

ideology
idiosyncrasy
idle (inactive)
idol (image)
illicit (forbidden)
  elicit
impermeable
imprimatur
inadvertent
incalculable
incessant
incidentally
incumbent
independent
indictment
indispensable
infrared

innocuous
innuendo
inoculate
insecticide
intermittent
interrupt
intravenous
iridescent
irrelevant
irresistible
irrigate
island

J

janitor
jeopardize
jewellery, jewelry
joule
journey
judgment
junta

K

khaki
kibbutz
kilometre, kilometer
kilowatt
knowledge

L

label
labyrinth
laissez faire
laser
league
legislature
leisure
leukemia

liable
liaison
libel
licence — noun
license — verb
lieutenant
lightning
likable
likelihood
liquefy
liquor
litre, liter
logarithm
logistics
lunar

M

mahogany
maintain
maintenance
malignant
mandatory
manoeuvre
maraschino
margarine
marijuana
  (or marihuana)
marital
marshal
massacre
mathematics
matrix
mayonnaise
mediocre
megabyte
megawatt
memento

menstruation
metaphor
metastasize
metric
microfiche
micrometer
microprocessor
migraine
mileage
milieu
milligram
millimetre,
  millimeter
minestrone
miniature
minuscule
minutiae
miscellaneous
mischievous
missile
misspell
mnemonic
moccasin
modem
molecular
monaural
monetary
monitor
morass
mortgage
mosquito
mustache
myopia

N

naive
narcissism

necessary
neither
neophyte
nickel
niece
noxious
nozzle
nuance
nuclear

O

obesity
occasion
occurrence
odyssey
ombudsman
omelet
omniscient
ophthalmologist
opiate
orgy
oscillator
overrun

P

panacea
parallel
paralyze
parameter
paraphernalia
paraplegic
parliament
parochial
pasteurized
percolator
per diem
peremptory

perennial
perimeter
peripheral
permissible
perquisite
personnel
perspiration
pertinent
pharmaceutical
phase (aspect)
  faze
Philippines
phosphorus
physician
physics
pinnacle
plebiscite
pneumonia
poisonous
pollutant
polyester
polymer
porcelain
porous
Portuguese
posthumous
potpourri
prairie
precede
precious
preferred
prerogative
prevalent
privilege
procedure
proceed

propeller
prophecy (noun)
prophesy (verb)
protein
protocol
proxy
pseudonym
psychology
ptomaine
publicly

Q

quasi
questionnaire
queue
quiche
quixotic

R

radar
rapport
rarefy
rebuttal
recede
receipt
receive
receptacle
recession
reciprocal
recommend
reconnaissance
recuperate
recurrence
referred
rehearsal
relevant
religious

remembrance
renege
rescind
resistance
restaurant
resuscitate
rhetoric
rheumatism
rhythm
robotics
roentgen
rotor

S

saboteur
saccharin (noun)
sacrilegious
salmon
satellite
savvy
scenario
schedule
scissors
secretary
seizure
separate
sergeant
siege
sieve
silhouette
similar
simultaneous
sinecure
sinus
siphon
skeptical, sceptical
sophomore

spaghetti
stratagem
strategy
stupefy
subpoena, subpena
subterranean
subtle
succeed
succinct
suffrage
superintendent
supersede
supervisor
surprise
surveillance
syllable
synagogue
synonymous
synopsis
syntax
syphilis

T

tariff
therapy
thief
threshold
tobacco
tongue
toxin
trafficking
tranquilizer
trauma
treasurer
trek
tyranny

U

ubiquitous
umbilical
unanimous
unerring
unnecessary
unprecedented
usage

V

vacillation
vacuum
vehicle
vengeance
verbatim
versatile
veterinarian
vice versa
vicious
vicissitude
villain
visitor

W

waiver
weird
wholly
withheld
womb
woolen

Y

yield

Z

zucchini

BIBLIOGRAPHY

Boston, Bruce O. *STET! Tricks of the Trade for Writers and Editors.* Alexandria, VA: Editorial Experts, Inc., 1986.

The Canadian Press Caps and Spelling. Toronto: The Canadian Press, 1993.

The Canadian Press Stylebook. Toronto: The Canadian Press, 1993.

Chapman, Robert L., editor. *Roget's International Thesaurus.* New York: HarperCollins Ltd., 5th edition, 1992.

Chicago Manual of Style. Chicago: University of Chicago Press, 14th edition, 1993.

Freelance Editors' Association of Canada. *Editing Canadian English.* Vancouver: Douglas and McIntyre Ltd., 1987.

Johnson, Edward D. *The Handbook of Good English.* New York: Washington Square Press, 1991.

Merriam-Webster's Secretarial Handbook. Springfield, MA: G&C Merriam Co., 3rd edition, 1993.

Miller, Casey and Kate Swift. *The Handbook of Non-sexist Writing.* New York: HarperCollins Ltd., 1988.

Murray, Donald. *Writing For Your Readers: Notes on the Writer's Craft from the Boston Globe.* Chester, CT: Globe Pequot, 2nd edition, 1992.

Parker, Roger C. *Looking Good in Print.* Alexandria, VA: Tools of the Trade, 1992.

Sabin, William A. *The Gregg Reference Manual.* Glencoe, IL: Gregg Division/McGraw-Hill Book Co., 7th edition, 1992.

Shaw, Harry. *Punctuate it Right!* New York: HarperCollins Ltd., 1994.

Tarrant, John. *Business Writing With Style*. New York: John Wiley Ltd., 1991.

Tarshis, Barry. *Grammar for Short People*. New York: Pocket Books, 1992.

Venolia, Jan. *Rewrite Right!* Berkeley, CA: Ten Speed Press, 1987.

Venolia, Jan. *Better Letters: A Handbook of Business and Personal Correspondence*. Berkeley, CA: Ten Speed Press, 1982.

Weiner, Ed. *Desktop Publishing Made Simple*. Garden City, NY: Doubleday Co. Ltd., 1991.

DICTIONARIES

The American Heritage Dictionary of the English Language. American Heritage, New York.

The Concise Oxford Dictionary of Current English. London: Oxford University Press.

Funk & Wagnalls Standard College Dictionary. Funk & Wagnalls, Canadian ed., Fitzhenry and Whiteside, Toronto

The Gage Canadian Dictionary. Gage Educational Publishing Limited, Toronto.

The Random House Dictionary of the English Language. Random House, New York.

Webster's Third New International Dictionary. G&C Merriam, Springfield, MA.

INDEX

Note: *Italicized words refer to the section entitled* Confused and Abused Words, *pp.* 89

132

OTHER TITLES IN THE
SELF-COUNSEL SERIES

PRACTICAL TIME MANAGEMENT
How to get more things done in less time
by Bradley C. McRae

Here is sound advice for anyone who needs to develop practical time management skills. It is designed to help any busy person, from any walk of life, use his or her time more effectively. Not only does it explain how to easily get more things done, it shows you how your self-esteem will improve in doing so. More important, emphasis is placed on maintenance so that you remain in control. Whether you want to find extra time to spend with your family or read the latest best-seller, this book will give you the guidance you need — without taking up a lot of your time! $7.95

Some of the skills you will learn are:

- Learning to monitor where your time goes

- Setting realistic and attainable goals

- Overcoming inertia

- Rewarding yourself

- Planning time with others

- Managing leisure time

- Finding time for physical fitness

- Planning time for hobbies and vacations

- Maintaining the new you

EFFECTIVE SPEAKING FOR BUSINESS SUCCESS
Making presentations, using audio-visuals, and more
by Jacqueline Dunckel and
Elizabeth Parnham

Give dynamic speeches, presentations, and media interviews. When you are called upon to speak in front of your business colleagues, or asked to represent your company in front of the media, do you communicate your thoughts effectively? Or do you become tongue-tied, nervous, and worry about misrepresenting yourself and your business?

Effective communication has always been the key to business success, and this book provides a straightforward approach to developing techniques to improve your on-the-job speaking skills. This book is as easy to pick up and use as a quick reference for a specific problem as it is to read from cover to cover. Whether you want to know how to deal with the media, when to use visual aids in a presentation, or how to prepare for chairing a meeting, this book will answer your questions and help you regain your confidence. $8.95

Contents include:

- Preparing your presentation

- When and where will you speak?

- Let's look at visual aids

- Let's hear what you have to say: rehearsing

- How do you sound?

THE COMPLETE GUIDE TO CANADIAN UNIVERSITIES
How to select a university and succeed when you get there
by Kevin Paul, M.A.

Whether you are still in high school or thinking about returning to school, the decision to go to university is a crucial one.

This book helps you make those decisions by detailing each step along the way — from getting information about schools and programs that interest you, to the best way to be organized and succeed in you course work. Detailed and up-to-date profiles of the universities are provided as well as exercises to help you pinpoint your goals and interests. $14.95

Questions answered include:

- How do I know if a university education is right for me?

- What are the benefits of having a university degree?

- What's the best way to study and stay motivated?

- Are there universities that offer degree programs by correspondence?

- What are the admission requirements for international students?

- What happens after I get my degree?

This new, revised edition includes chapters on co-op education programs and how universities are addressing the concerns of women and special needs students.

ORDERING INFORMATION

All prices are subject to change without notice. Books are available in book, department, and stationery stores. If you cannot buy the book through a store, please use this order form. (Please print)

Please send your order to the nearest location:
Self-Counsel Press, 1481 Charlotte Road
North Vancouver, B.C. V7J 1H1

Self-Counsel Press, 8-2283 Argentia Road
Mississauga, Ontario L5N 5Z2

Name _____

Address _____

_____

Charge to:
❑ Visa   ❑ MasterCard

Account Number _____

Validation Date _____ Expiry Date _____

Signature _____

❑Check here for a free catalogue outlining all of our publications.

Please add $3.00 for postage and handling. Please add GST to your book order.

YES, please send me:

_____copies of **Practical Time Management**, $7.95

_____copies of **Effective Speaking For Business Success**, $8.95

_____copies of **The Complete Guide to Canadian Universities**, $14.95

_____copies of **Write Right!** $7.95